DIABETIC AIR FRYER COOKBOOK

Becca Russell

© Copyright 2022 - All rights reserved.

This document is aimed at providing accurate and reliable information regarding the subject at hand. The publication is sold because the publisher is not obligated to provide qualified, officially permitted or otherwise accountable services. If any advice is necessary, whether legal or professional, it should be ordered from a person with experience in the profession.

In no way is it legal to reproduce, duplicate, or transmit any part of this document in either electronic means or printed format. Recording of this publication is strictly prohibited and any storage of this document is not allowed unless with written permission from the publisher.

TABLE OF CONTENTS

CHAPTER 1. INTRODUCTION 8
I. Prediabetes VS type 2 diabetes. 9
II. The top 10 causes of diabetes 10
III. What is an air fryer? 12
IV. 3 reasons why you should be cooking with an air fryer (especially if you have diabetes) 12
V. 10 foods and beverages to remove from your shopping list 13
VI. Diabetic-friendly foods 15
VII. Conclusion 17

CHAPTER 2. BREAKFAST 19
1. Cocoa Pudding 20
2. Lemon Biscotti 20
3. Chia Pie 21
4. Ricotta Muffins 21
5. Sweet Baked Avocado 22
6. Rhubarb Pie 22
7. Lemon Pie 23
8. Baked Cantaloupe 23
9. Sweet Carambola Chips 24
10. Spiced Nuts 24
11. Pancakes 25
12. Baked Eggs 25
13. Tofu Scramble 26
14. Sweet Corn Fritters with Avocado 26
15. Blueberry Muffins 27
16. Homemade Muffins 28

CHAPTER 3. FISH RECIPES 29
17. Easy Tuna Wraps 30
18. Asian-Inspired Swordfish Steaks 30
19. Salmon with Fennel and Carrot 31
20. Ranch Tilapia fillets 31
21. Asian Sesame Cod 32
22. Lemon Scallops with Asparagus 32
23. Chilean Sea Bass with Green Olive Relish 33
24. Ginger and Green Onion Fish 34

TABLE OF CONTENTS

25. Fish Tacos 35
26. Spicy Cajun Shrimp 35
27. Quick Shrimp Scampi 36
28. Fish and Vegetable Tacos 36
29. Snapper with Fruit 37
30. Tuna and Fruit Kebabs 37
31. Stevia Lemon Snapper with Fruit 38
32. Breaded Hake with Green Chili Pepper and Mayonnaise 38

CHAPTER 4. BEEF RECIPES 39
33. Roast Beef 40
34. Beef Empanadas 40
35. Flavored Rib Eye Steak 41
36. Steak 42
37. Chinese Steak and Broccoli 42
38. Mustard Marinated Beef 43
39. Beef Korma Curry 43
40. Low-fat Steak 44
41. Beef with Mushrooms 44
42. Beef Schnitzel 45
43. Beef Steak Kabobs with Vegetables 45
44. Beef Scallops 46

CHAPTER 5. PORK RECIPES 47
45. Ranch Pork Chops 48
46. Glazed Pork Shoulder 48
47. Pork Shoulder with Pineapple Sauce 49
48. Bacon Wrapped Pork Tenderloin 50
49. Pork Tenderloin with Bell Peppers 50
50. Pork Loin with Potatoes 51
51. Pork Spare Ribs 51
52. BBQ Pork Ribs 52
53. Pork Fillets with Serrano Ham 52
54. Pork in a Blanket 53
55. Provencal Ribs 53
56. Marinated Loin Potatoes 54
57. Pork Bondiola Chop 54

TABLE OF CONTENTS

58. Pork Tenderloin 55
59. Roast Pork 55
60. Fried Pork Chops 56
61. Creamy Pork 56
62. Mesquite Pork Chops 57

CHAPTER 6. LAMB RECIPES 58
63. Juicy Lamb Chops 59
64. Crispy Lamb 59
65. Lamb and Creamy Brussels Sprouts 60
66. Rosemary Lamb Chops 60
67. Za'atar Lamb Loin Chops 61
68. Spiced Lamb Steaks 61

CHAPTER 7. POULTRY RECIPES 62
69. Soy Chicken and Sesame 63
70. Chicken Fajitas with Avocados 63
71. Herbed Chicken Marsala 64
72. Greek Chicken Kebabs 65
73. Stevia Lemon Garlic Chicken 66
74. Chicken with Provencal Herbs and Potatoes 66
75. Baked Lemon Pepper Chicken Drumsticks 67
76. Balsamic Glazed Chicken 68
77. Chicken Alfredo 69
78. Rolls Stuffed with Broccoli and Carrots with Chicken 70
79. Spicy Chicken Strips 71
80. Baked Tomato Chicken 71
81. Chicken in Tomato Juice 72
82. Chicken Wings with Curry 72
83. Chicken Meatballs 73
84. Air Fryer Chicken Wings 73
85. Spicy Chicken Meatballs 74
86. Salted Biscuit Pie Turkey Chops 74
87. Chicken Wings 75
88. Mini Turkey Meatballs 76

DIABETIC AIR FRYER COOKBOOK • 5

TABLE OF CONTENTS

CHAPTER 8. SNACK RECIPES 77
89. Zucchini Crisps 78
90. Skinny Pumpkin Chips 78
91. Air Fried Ripe Plantains 79
92. Air Fried Plantains in Coconut Sauce 79
93. Cinnamon Pear Chips 80
94. Air fryer Chicken Nuggets 80
95. Air fryer Sweet Potato Fries 81
96. Air fryer Kale Chips 81
97. Spiced Apples 82
98. Cinnamon Toasted Almonds 82
99. Avocado Fries with Roasted Garlic Mayonnaise 83
100. Chili Fingerling Potatoes 84

CHAPTER 9. VEGETABLE AND VEGETARIAN RECIPES 85
101. Delicata Squash 86
102. Spicy Glazed Carrots 86
103. Corn on the Cob with Herb 'Butter' 87
104. Sesame Seeds Bok Choy 87
105. Sweet-and-Sour Mixed Veggies 88
106. Roast Eggplant and Zucchini Bites 88
107. Basil Tomatoes 89
108. Stuffed Tomatoes 89
109. Spicy Potatoes 90
110. Roasted Okra 90
111. Hasselback Potatoes 91
112. Glazed Carrots 91
113. Spicy Green Beans 92
114. Soy Sauce Mushrooms 92
115. Braised Mushrooms 93
116. Lemony Spinach 93
117. Buffalo Cauliflower Wings 94
118. Sweet Potato Cauliflower Patties 95
119. Fried Peppers with Sriracha Mayo 96
120. Spicy Roasted Potatoes 96
121. Okra 97
122. Cauliflower Rice 98

TABLE OF CONTENTS

123. Asparagus Avocado Soup 99
124. Roasted Broccoli with Sesame Seeds..............100
125. Crispy Tofu...100
126. Kale with Pine Nuts 101
127. Spiced Sweet Potatoes 101
128. Glazed Broccoli..102
129. Green Beans with Carrots 103
130. Broccoli with Cauliflower 103
131. Mushroom with Green Peas 104
132. Carrot with Zucchini...104
133. Potato with Bell Peppers 105
134. Veggie Ratatouille...106
135. Seasoned Veggies 106
136. Balsamic Veggies 107
137. Maple Glazed Veggies..108
138. Stuffed Eggplants 109
139. Green Beans & Mushroom Casserole...............110
140. Beans & Rice Stuffed Bell Peppers...................110
141. Rice & Veggie Stuffed Tomatoes.......................111
142. Oats & Beans Stuffed Bell Peppers 112
143. Beans & Veggie Burgers 113
144. Veggie Fried Rice..113
145. Chickpeas Falafel..114
146. Tofu in Orange Sauce...115
147. Tofu with Cauliflower..116
148. Tofu with Broccoli 116
149. Classic Fried Pickles...117
150. Japanese Tempura Bowl 118
151. Crispy Roasted Broccoli.....................................119
152. Crispy Jalapeno Coins..119
153. Cauliflower Casserole..120
154. Artichoke Hearts 121
155. Basil Eggplant Casserole 121
156. Brussels Sprouts and Broccoli 122
157. Easy Frizzled Leeks..122
158. Fried Green Beans with Pecorino Romano.....123

CHAPTER 10. 21-DAY MEAL PLAN..............124

Chapter 1
INTRODUCTION

Sadly, the world is plagued with many different diseases.

One of these causes 100,000 deaths each year in the United States alone.

And it's a steadily increasing number, recent studies show.

Suffice it to say, it is among the top 7 causes of death in our country.

Scientists also claim that unless we do something about it, by 2025 there will be a 33% increase in deaths due to this "silent killer".

What am I talking about?

I'm talking about type 2 diabetes.

Just think that about 96 million Americans - more than 1 in 3 - have prediabetes, the condition that precedes the disease.

And the disconcerting news is that 80% of people with prediabetes don't even know they have it.

This is a problem because diabetics are 94% more likely to have cancer and strokes than healthy people.

Scary numbers, I know – but fear not, because I also have some good news for you.

As a matter of fact, here you will find how to prevent and curb the disease, whether you have prediabetes or type 2 diabetes, through dietary strategies that I will explain later.

But that's not all.

Because you will also learn how, thanks to one kitchen gadget, you will be able to enjoy your favorite foods without resorting to starvation diets and even without forsaking your favorite dishes.

On top of that, you will also learn which 10 foods you should avoid, which foods to eat, and the 10 diabetes-causing factors that you absolutely must know about.

Are you ready?

Let's dive right into it.

I. Prediabetes VS type 2 diabetes.

While they may sound like the same thing, they certainly are not.

Let me elaborate further.

To start with, both share the same problem: high blood glucose levels.

How does this happen?

It's quite straightforward.

You must know that insulin – the hormone produced by the pancreas – is responsible for transporting glucose into the cells to be used as an energy source.

But when insulin fails to deliver glucose into the cells, insulin resistance occurs.

So, what does the pancreas do?

It produces more insulin than usual, to try and persuade the cells to absorb glucose.

In this case, when the body fails to use insulin well, this buildup of sugars fails to enter the cells and is transported right into the bloodstream.

Simply put, this is the case with prediabetes or type 2 diabetes.

Now, let's see what the differences between the two are instead:

- **Prediabetes**: When you have prediabetes, it means that your blood sugar levels are higher than average, but still not enough to call it diabetes.

According to a study published in Pubmed, not everyone who has prediabetes will develop diabetes, but most people will. We are talking about 70% of the cases.

But the good news is that it can be prevented through some nutritional strategies that I will be revealing shortly.

Furthermore, the latest guidelines recommend using the term *glucose intolerance*, rather than prediabetes. This is because – although as we saw just now, the risks are high – it is still not full-blown diabetes.

When do we speak of prediabetes?

When the blood sugar level is between 100 and 125 mg/dl.

- **Type 2 diabetes**: This is when blood sugar levels are high. Namely, when they exceed 126 mg/dl. That's why this condition is known as hyperglycemia.

The cause is that in this situation insulin works poorly, and as mentioned before, it results in a very high accumulation of glucose in the blood.

Additionally, having type 2 diabetes poses very high risks of the emergence of cardiovascular disease and other types of health disorders.

Are there any possible solutions?

The answer is YES! Actually, by continuing to read this book, you will be able to understand how to prevent and even push diabetes into remission. More on that later.

But first, in the next section, I want to discuss the possible causes of diabetes – and how to fight them before it's too late.

II. THE TOP 10 CAUSES OF DIABETES

Several factors increase the risk of prediabetes and diabetes.

In this part, we shall see that the risk factors fall into 2 categories.

But first, we need to know what could be the early symptoms – or the first "red flags" of diabetes.

Why is it crucial to know them?

Because one in four people with diabetes doesn't yet know they have it. This means about 7 million Americans.

What are these symptoms then?

Let's examine them below:

- increased hunger
- increased thirst
- weight loss
- frequent urination
- blurred vision
- extreme fatigue
- sores that do not heal

Usually, the symptoms can be the result of bad habits that we have in our lives. That's why it's so important to take timely action if you want to prevent diabetes or send it into remission.

Now as promised, let's see the 2 categories of risk factors:

1. Factors beyond your control:

Family history: if people in your family have had diabetes, then you are at greater risk of developing it.

Age: the older you are, the higher the risk of prediabetes and type 2 diabetes. Type 2 diabetes usually occurs in middle-aged adults, most often 40+.

2. Factors that depend on you and that you can act upon instead:

Weight: being overweight or obese increases the risk of developing diabetes. Losing 5% to 10% of your body weight, together with regular exercise, can significantly reduce the risk you run of developing diabetes.

Physical activity: lack of exercise is a key risk factor for prediabetes and type 2 diabetes. Regular physical activity helps to reduce insulin resistance. This means that your body can use your insulin more effectively.

Blood pressure: besides causing damage to the cardiovascular system, hypertension is linked to some complications of diabetes. People with diabetes should keep their blood pressure below 130/80 mm Hg.

Cholesterol (lipid) levels: diabetes is associated with atherosclerosis (hardening of the arteries) and other blood vessel diseases. Low cholesterol or high triglycerides can increase the risk of type 2 diabetes and cardiovascular disease.

Smoking: smoking is proven to damage many different organs including pancreatic function.

Alcohol: heavy alcohol intake can trigger pancreatic inflammation and limit the pancreas's ability to produce enough insulin.

Stress: stress management is an important component of a healthy life, not only for diabetes but also for heart disease and many other conditions. Find a way to deal with the sources of your stress and make time for the things you love.

Diet: it's important to eat healthy foods in the right amounts. Diet is one of the biggest modifiable risk factors for prediabetes and type 2 diabetes.

And speaking of diet...

Let me now introduce you to what has become an indispensable tool in the kitchens of diabetics, and how they have been able to keep on eating their favorite dishes thanks to this new way of cooking.

What am I talking about?

The Air Fryer.

III. WHAT IS AN AIR FRYER?

Recent studies indicate that people suffering from diabetes or having prediabetes should eliminate deep-fried foods from their diet.

Why is that?

Because deep-fried foods dramatically increase your chances of developing diabetes and cardiovascular disease.

But that's not all, because according to one study by the Harvard School of Public Health, overconsumption of fried foods is a high-risk factor for obesity in adults – and as we saw earlier, obesity promotes diabetes.

This is partly due to the large amount of oil that is used for deep-frying.

Indeed, cooking oil tends to break down during frying, causing a chemical transformation that changes the fatty acid composition of the oil.

During this oil degradation, foods tend to absorb fatty acids, and as a consequence, you are likely to gain weight, increase cholesterol levels, and have blood pressure issues.

That's why air fryers have become the best solution in the kitchen.

But let's see what they are and how they work.

The air fryer – also known as an oil-free fryer - is an electric appliance capable of frying food without fats (oil or butter) but just thanks to its heat.

In fact, cooking food with an air fryer enables you to use less oil while still getting the same consistency and flavor as deep-fried food.

Not only that, you can cook almost any dish with your air fryer and preserve all the nutritional properties of the ingredients, which does not happen with classic deep-frying.

One thing needs mentioning: it is not accurate to claim that air fryers do not use oil for frying. In some dishes they do, but not always.

In fact, just a spoonful (or a drizzle) of oil is usually sufficient, because it is the hot air that does all the work.

This eliminates as much as 80% of the oil fats, resulting in fewer calories.

But that's not the end of it, because there are other advantages to opting for air fryer cooking.

IV. 3 REASONS WHY YOU SHOULD BE COOKING WITH AN AIR FRYER (ESPECIALLY IF YOU HAVE DIABETES)

This is really important so let's see what the 3 reasons are:

1. Air fryers reduce the amount of acrylamide in food.

Deep-fried foods contain high amounts of acrylamide – a substance that forms when carbohydrates are heated to high temperatures – which has been linked to heart disease.

In fact, the *Department of Health and Human Services* defines acrylamide as "carcinogenic to humans" and based on recent animal studies, they have concluded that this can even lead to cancer.

However, more research is needed, according to the National Cancer Institute.

What's the good news?

Air fryers actually seem to produce lower amounts of acrylamide. Indeed, a 2015 study published in the Journal of Food Science found that air-fried fries had 90% less acrylamide than deep-fried fries.

2. Air fryers reduce calories

As mentioned before, another advantage of air fryers is that they reduce calories, because they don't require as much oil.

For example, air-fried foods can require only one teaspoon of oil – that's just 40 calories.

Conversely, a single tablespoon of oil absorbed into food during ordinary frying adds about 120 calories. Therefore, replacing deep-fried foods with air-fried foods can help with weight management.

3. Air fryers do not produce some of the toxic compounds found in deep-fried foods

There is another benefit made possible by reducing oil use.

For example, when oil is reused for deep-frying (as often happens in restaurants), its quality decreases, depleting the food of antioxidants and producing harmful chemicals. Therefore, eating foods without antioxidants compromises the body's antioxidant defense system, increasing the risk of disease.

It may also cause inflammation of the blood vessels (which reduces the blood flow) and hypertension.

This far, you've seen what an air fryer is, how it works, and why you should use it.

In the next section, we'll go back to food choices related to diabetes, and especially what foods you should delete from your shopping list – and why.

V. 10 FOODS AND BEVERAGES TO REMOVE FROM YOUR SHOPPING LIST

1. Sugary drinks.

Sugary drinks are harmful to diabetic patients since they are very high in carbohydrates

In fact, a 12-ounce (354 ml) can of Coke, contains 38.5 grams of carbs.

Similarly, sweetened iced tea contains almost 45 grams of carbohydrates.

Plus these beverages are rich in fructose, which is strongly linked to insulin resistance and diabetes.

2. Trans Fat.

Fats are bad for your diabetes.

Specifically, they are related to increased inflammation, insulin resistance, and belly fat, as well as lower levels of HDL (good) cholesterol and reduced arterial function.

Did you know that trans fats are banned in most countries? And in 2018 the Food and Drug Administration (FDA) banned the use of partially hydrogenated oil, which is the main source of trans fats.

3. White bread, rice, and pasta.

Eating bread, bagels, and other refined flour foods has been shown to significantly increase blood sugar levels in people with type 1 and type 2 diabetes.

In one study, gluten-free kinds of pasta were also found to increase blood sugar, with rice-based varieties having the greatest effect

4. Fruit yogurt.

Plain yogurt can be a good option for people with diabetes. However, fruit yogurt is a different story.

In fact, flavored yogurts are typically made with skimmed or lean milk but they are loaded with carbohydrates and sugar.

Therefore, a 1-cup (245 grams) serving of fruit yogurt may contain up to 31 grams of sugar, which means that nearly 61% of its calories come from sugar.

5. Breakfast cereals.

Choosing to have cereals in the morning can be one of the worst ways to start your day if you have diabetes.

Despite the health benefits claimed on their boxes, most cereals are highly processed and contain way more carbs and sugars than many people think.

Besides, they provide very little protein, a nutrient that can make you feel full and satisfied while keeping your blood sugar levels stable throughout the day.

6. Coffee drinks.

(Bitter) coffee has been linked to numerous health benefits, including a reduced risk of diabetes.

However, caution should be applied when it comes to drinking coffee-flavored beverages. Why so? Again, because they're loaded with carbs.

For example, a 16-ounce (473 ml) Starbucks Caramel Frappuccino contains 57 grams of carbohydrates.

7. Honey.

People with diabetes tend to cut down on white sugar. However, other forms of sugar can also cause blood sugar spikes. These include brown sugar and "natural" sugars such as honey, as well as agave nectar and maple syrup.

Although these sweeteners are not highly processed, they contain at least as many carbohydrates like white sugar.

Your best strategy is to avoid all forms of

sugar and use low-carb natural sweeteners instead - or better still, none at all.

8. Packaged snacks.

Snacking on pretzels, crackers or other packaged savory snacks is not healthy for people with prediabetes or diabetes.

In fact, these products are generally made from refined flour and provide few nutrients, while having many fast-digesting carbohydrates that can rapidly spike blood sugar.

Just think, one study found that snacks provide an average of 7.7% more carbohydrates than what they claim on their labels. And depending on the size of the packaging, controlling the portion of these snacks that they eat is a challenge for lots of people.

9. Fruit juices.

Despite fruit juice being perceived as a healthy drink, its effects on blood sugar are similar to those of soft drinks and other sugary drinks.

This is true both for 100% unsweetened fruit juices and for types that contain added sugars. In some cases, fruit juice is even richer in sugars and carbs than soda drinks.

For example, 8 ounces (250 ml) of soda and apple juice contain 22 and 24 grams of sugar, respectively. An equivalent serving of grape juice provides as much as 35 grams of sugar.

10. French fries.

French fries are a food you should stay away from, particularly if you have diabetes.

To start with, potatoes are rich in carbs. An average potato contains 34.8 grams of carbohydrates, 2.4 of which come from fiber.

However, once peeled and deep-fried in vegetable oil, potatoes can do much worse than just increasing blood sugar.

Actually, as you've seen before, several studies link frequent consumption of fries and other fried foods to heart disease and cancer.

That's why choosing to cook with an air fryer may be the best choice you can make.

Now that you have seen what foods and drinks to avoid, in the last part you will discover the "friendly" foods that you can include in your diet without worries.

VI. DIABETIC-FRIENDLY FOODS

There is no specific diet for diabetic patients. However, sticking to a diet that helps regulate blood sugar levels is certainly the best choice you can make.

Furthermore, knowing which foods are your allies can reduce the risk of such complications as nerve damage and heart disease, as well as counteract obesity and prevent possible strokes.

Plus, the foods I am going to disclose in a moment can help reduce cholesterol levels to support heart health, improve blood sugar management, and help you feel satiated for a longer time, to avoid eating when you are not really hungry.

Are you ready to discover what they are?

Great, let's get started:

Leafy greens.

Green leafy vegetables are rich in vitamins, minerals, and essential nutrients. They also have minimal impact on blood sugar levels.

Leafy greens include:

- Spinach

- Broccoli
- Green cabbage
- Beet greens
- Dark leaf salads
- Watercress
- Arugula
- Bok choy
- Kale

Wholegrain cereals.

Whole grains are high in fiber content and provide more nutrients than refined white grains.

Eating a high-fiber diet is important for people with diabetes because fibers slow down the digestion process. Slower absorption of nutrients helps keep blood sugar levels stable.

Examples of whole grains to include in your diet are:

- Brown rice
- Wholemeal bread
- Wholegrain pasta
- Buckwheat
- Quinoa
- Millet
- Bulgar wheat
- Rye

Fatty fish.

Fatty fish is great for any diet. That's because it contains valuable omega-3 fatty acids. These are known as EPA and DHA.

The ADA reports that a diet rich in polyunsaturated and monounsaturated fats can improve blood glucose and lipid control in people with diabetes.

Some fish are a plentiful source of both polyunsaturated and monounsaturated fats. They include:

- Salmon
- Mackerel
- Sardines
- Albacore tuna
- Herring
- Trout

Beans.

Beans are a great option for people with diabetes. This is because they are a source of vegetable protein and can satisfy your appetite by helping you reduce your carbohydrate intake.

Beans are also low in the glycemic index (GI) and are better at regulating glycemia than many other starch-rich foods.

In fact, according to a report by North Dakota State University, beans can also help people manage their blood sugar levels. They are complex carbohydrates, so the body digests them more slowly than other carbohydrates.

Among the many types of beans are:

- Kidney
- Pinto
- Black
- Adzuki

Nuts.

Nuts can be another excellent addition to your diet. Like fish, nuts contain fatty acids that help keep your heart healthy.

Walnuts are particularly rich in a type of omega-3 called alpha-lipoic acid (ALA). Like other omega-3s, ALA is important for heart health. Diabetics may have a higher risk of heart disease and stroke, so it is important for them to consume these fatty acids.

One study suggested that eating walnuts is linked to a lower incidence of diabetes.

Dairy products.

Dairy products contain essential nutrients, including calcium and protein. Some research suggests that dairy products have a positive effect on insulin secretion in some individuals with type 2 diabetes.

Some dairy products you can add to your diet are:

- Parmesan or ricotta cheese
- Low-fat or skimmed milk
- Low-fat Greek or plain yogurt

Berries.

Berries are rich in antioxidants, which can help prevent oxidative stress. Oxidative stress is linked to a wide range of health conditions, including heart disease and some types of cancer.

Besides, studies have found chronic levels of oxidative stress in people with diabetes. This occurs when there is an imbalance in the body between antioxidants and unstable molecules called free radicals.

Berries contain high levels of antioxidants and fiber, plus Vitamin C,

- Vitamin C
- Vitamin K
- Manganese
- Potassium

Berries include

- Blueberries
- Blackberries
- Strawberries
- Raspberries

Chia seeds.

Experts agree that chia seeds are a superfood because of their high content of antioxidants and omega-3s. They are also a good source of plant protein and fiber.

In a 2017 study, people who were overweight and had type 2 diabetes lost more weight after 6 months when they included chia seeds in their diet, compared to those who consumed an oat bran alternative.

Therefore, researchers believe that chia seeds can help people manage type 2 diabetes.

VII. Conclusion

We have reached the end of this first section and I know you really want to see what recipes I have for you.

But first let's recap.

You now know the main differences between diabetes and prediabetes.

You have seen their main causes and which symptoms to watch out for.

Plus you now understand how an air fryer can be your ally in the kitchen to prepare tasty dishes with that satisfying crunch that you can eat even with diabetes.

You also know which foods are your friends, and which to avoid.

Now the time has come to explore the recipes I have compiled for you.

I know the recipes will inspire you, but sometimes we all get stuck cooking the same things from habit.

So before you dive into those recipes, let me just explain how you can enjoy a healthy, varied diet for more than 1000 days – it is so simple.

Most people have breakfast, and two main meals a day, and sometimes a snack too.

One of the secrets to a healthy diet is making sure you have variety, and making sure you have plenty of fruit and vegetables each day – in fact experts recommend 5 portions of fruit and vegetables per day.

If you are diabetic, you need to manage your sugar intake, and so need to be very careful about which fruits you consume, and how much quantity. For that reason, instead of lots of fruit options, I have instead given you a large variety of vegetable dishes, so that you can make sure you get your 5 a day easily, but based primarily on vegetables.

You should also make sure that you balance your consumption of red meats – beef, lamb and pork – with white meats, including chicken and fish, so I have made sure I have given you an equal balance of recipes for those protein groups.

So to create an interesting and varied diet, just create combinations of the vegetable dishes to go with fish and meat for your main meals.

You have 36 recipes for lamb, pork and beef and another 36 recipes for poultry and fish. Let's just say you choose red meat one of your main meals and poultry and fish for your other. You have 58 vegetable dishes, so with half of those recipes prepared for lunch and the other half for dinner, that's two sets of 29 recipes. With that number of recipes, you can have a different combination every day for an incredible 1044 days without eating the same combination twice!

The choice is up to you of course, but it really is that simple to give yourself an interesting healthy and varied diet, even with diabetes.

So let's get started. Read and get inspired by the choices available with your air fryer and enjoy your food!

Chapter 2
BREAKFAST

1
Cocoa Pudding

10 minutes | 20 minutes | 8

Ingredients

- 2 cups ricotta cheese
- 2 tablespoons coconut flour
- 3 tablespoons Splenda
- 3 eggs, beaten
- 1 tablespoon vanilla extract
- ½ cup coconut cream
- 1 tablespoon cocoa powder

Directions

1. Whisk the coconut cream with cocoa powder.
2. Then add eggs, Splenda, ricotta cheese, and coconut flour.
3. Mix the mixture until smooth and pour in the air fryer.
4. Cook the pudding at 350F for 20 minutes. Stir the pudding every 5 minutes during cooking.

Nutrition: Calories: 112; Carbohydrates: 2.1 g; Fats: 8 g; Protein: 6.4 g

2
Lemon Biscotti

15 minutes | 40 minutes | 6

Ingredients

- 2 oz almonds, chopped
- 2 tablespoons coconut oil
- 2 eggs, beaten
- 1 teaspoon vanilla extract
- 1 cup coconut flour
- 1 teaspoon lemon zest, grated
- ½ teaspoon baking powder
- 1 teaspoon lemon juice
- ¼ cup coconut cream
- 1 teaspoon sesame oil
- 3 tablespoons Erythritol

Directions

1. Mix all ingredients in the mixing bowl.
2. Then knead the dough and put in the air fryer basket.
3. Cook the dough for 38 minutes at 375F.
4. Then slice the dough into biscotti and cook at 400F for 2 minutes more.

Nutrition: Calories: 178; Carbohydrates: 5.8 g; Fats: 15.2 g; Protein: 4.8 g

3
Chia Pie

10 minutes | 30 minutes | 8

Ingredients

- 1 cup almond flour
- 2 tablespoons chia seeds
- 4 eggs, beaten
- 4 tablespoons Erythritol
- 1 teaspoon vanilla extract
- 2 tablespoons coconut oil, melted

Directions

1. Brush the air fryer basket with coconut oil.
2. Then mix almond flour with chia seeds, eggs, vanilla extract, and Erythritol.
3. Put the mixture in the air fryer basket, flatten it into the shape of the pie and cook at 365F for 30 minutes.

Nutrition: Calories: 134; Carbohydrates: 3.7 g; Fats: 10.9 g; Protein: 6.1 g

4
Ricotta Muffins

15 minutes | 11 minutes | 4

Ingredients

- 4 teaspoons ricotta cheese
- 1 egg, beaten
- ½ teaspoon baking powder
- 1 teaspoon vanilla extract
- 8 teaspoons coconut flour
- 3 tablespoons coconut cream
- 2 teaspoons Erythritol
- Cooking spray

Directions

1. Spray the muffin molds with cooking spray.
2. Then mix all ingredients in the mixing bowl.
3. When you get a smooth batter, pour it in the muffin molds and place in the air fryer basket.
4. Cook the muffins at 365F for 11 minutes.

Nutrition: Calories: 75; Carbohydrates: 5.0 g; Fats: 4.6 g; Protein: 3.9 g

5
Sweet Baked Avocado

Ingredients

- 1 avocado, pitted, halved
- 2 teaspoons Erythritol
- 1 teaspoon vanilla extract
- 2 teaspoons butter

Directions

1. Sprinkle the avocado halves with Erythritol, vanilla extract, and butter.
2. Put the avocado halves in the air fryer and cook at 350F for 20 minutes.

Nutrition: Calories: 231; Carbohydrates: 2.9 g; Fats: 23.4 g; Protein: 2.2 g

6
Rhubarb Pie

Ingredients

- 4 oz rhubarb, chopped
- ¼ cup coconut cream
- 1 teaspoon vanilla extract
- ¼ cup Erythritol
- 1 cup coconut flour
- 1 egg, beaten
- 4 tablespoons coconut oil, softened

Directions

1. Mix coconut cream with vanilla extract, Erythritol, coconut flour, egg, and coconut oil.
2. When the mixture is smooth, add rhubarb and stir gently.
3. Pour the mixture in the air fryer and cook the pie at 375F for 20 minutes.
4. Cool the cooked pie and cut into servings.

Nutrition: Calories: 141; Carbohydrates: 5.9 g; Fats: 13.2 g; Protein: 2.4 g

7
Lemon Pie

Ingredients

- 1 cup coconut flour
- ½ lemon, sliced
- ¼ cup heavy cream
- 2 eggs, beaten
- 2 tablespoons Erythritol
- 1 teaspoon baking powder
- Cooking spray

Directions

1. Spray the air fryer basket with cooking spray.
2. Then line the bottom of the air fryer with lemon.
3. In the mixing bowl, mix coconut flour with heavy cream, eggs, Erythritol, and baking powder.
4. Pour the batter over the lemons and cook the pie at 365F for 35 minutes.

Nutrition: Calories: 95; Carbohydrates: 5.4 g; Fats: 6.7 g; Protein: 3.7 g

8
Baked Cantaloupe

Ingredients

- 1 cup cantaloupe, chopped
- 1 teaspoon vanilla extract
- 1 tablespoon Erythritol
- 1 teaspoon olive oil

Directions

1. Put the cantaloupe in the air fryer basket and sprinkle with vanilla extract, Erythritol, and olive oil.
2. Cook the dessert at 375F for 10 minutes.

Nutrition: Calories: 53 ; Carbohydrates: 6.6 g; Fats: 2.5 g; Protein: 0.7 g

9
Sweet Carambola Chips

Ingredients

- 10 oz carambola, sliced
- 1 teaspoon coconut oil, melted
- 1 tablespoon Erythritol

Directions

1. Mix the carambola with coconut oil and Erythritol.
2. Next, put it in the air fryer and cook at 340F for 50 minutes. Shake the carambola slices every 5 minutes.

Nutrition: Calories: 23; Carbohydrates: 3.2 g; Fats: 0.9 g; Protein: 0.5 g

10
Spiced Nuts

Ingredients

- 1 cup almonds
- 1 cup pecan halves
- 1 cup cashews
- 1 egg white, beaten
- ½ tsp cinnamon, ground
- Pinch cayenne pepper
- ¼ tsp cloves, ground
- A pinch of salt

Directions

1. Combine the egg white with spices. Preheat your air fryer to 300°F.
2. Toss the nuts in the spiced mixture. Cook for 25 minutes, stirring several times throughout the cooking time.

Nutrition: Calories: 240; Carbohydrates: 2.4 g; Fats: 23.1 g; Protein: 5.9 g

11 Pancakes

5 minutes | 6 minutes | 4

Ingredients

- 1 ½ cup coconut flour
- 1 tsp salt
- 1 tbsp olive oil
- 3 ½ tsp baking powder
- 1 tbsp Erythritol sweetener
- 1 ½ tsp baking soda
- 3 tbsp unsalted butter or grass-fed butter
- 1 ¼ cup reduced-fat milk
- 1 egg (pastured)

Directions

1. Switch on the Air fryer, insert the fryer pan and grease it with olive oil.
2. Next, close the lid, set the fryer to 220°F, and preheat for 5 minutes.
3. Meanwhile, take a medium bowl, add all the ingredients, whisk until well blended and then let the mixture rest for 5 minutes.
4. Open the fryer and pour in some of the pancake mixture as thinly as possible. Close the lid and cook for 6 minutes until nicely golden. Turn the pancake halfway through the frying.
5. When the Air fryer beeps, open the lid, transfer the pancake onto a serving plate and use the remaining batter for cooking more pancakes in the same way.
6. Serve straight away with fresh fruit slices.

Nutrition: Calories: 162; Carbohydrates: 16.2 g; Fats: 8.2 g; Protein: 5.7 g

12 Baked Eggs

5 minutes | 17 minutes | 2

Ingredients

- 2 tbsp frozen spinach, thawed
- ½ tsp salt
- ¼ tsp ground black pepper
- 2 eggs
- 3 tsp grated reduced-fat Parmesan cheese
- 2 tbsp reduced-fat milk

Directions

1. Switch on the Air fryer, insert the fryer basket, grease it with olive oil and then shut the lid.
2. Set the fryer at 330°F and preheat for 5 minutes.
3. Meanwhile, take 2 silicon muffin cups and grease them with oil. Then, crack an egg into each cup and evenly add cheese, spinach, and milk.
4. Season the egg with salt and black pepper and gently stir the ingredients without breaking the egg yolk.
5. Open the fryer and add muffin cups to it. Close the lid and cook for 8 to 12 minutes until the eggs are as done as you prefer.
6. When the Air fryer beeps, open its lid, take out the muffin cups and serve.

Nutrition: Calories: 103; Carbohydrates: 3.1 g; Fats: 5.4 g; Protein: 11.5 g

13
Tofu Scramble

 5 minutes   18 minutes   3

Ingredients

- 12 oz tofu, extra-firm, drained and cut into ½-inch cubed
- 1 tsp garlic powder
- 1 tsp onion powder
- 1 tsp paprika
- ½ tsp ground black pepper
- ½ tsp salt
- 1 tbsp olive oil
- 2 tsp xanthan gum

Directions

1. Switch on the Air fryer, insert the fryer basket and grease it with olive oil. Then close the lid, set the fryer to 220°F and preheat for 5 minutes.
2. Meanwhile, place tofu pieces in a bowl, drizzle with oil, sprinkle with xanthan gum, and toss until well coated.
3. Add the remaining ingredients to the tofu and then toss until well coated.
4. Open the fryer, add the tofu and close. Cook for 13 minutes until nicely golden and crispy, shaking the basket every 5 minutes.
5. When the Air fryer beeps, open the lid, transfer the tofu onto a serving plate and serve.

Nutrition: Calories: 129; Carbohydrates: 2.5 g; Fats: 8.3 g; Protein: 10.6 g

14
Sweet Corn Fritters with Avocado

 20 minutes   10 minutes   3

Ingredients

- 2 cups sweetcorn kernels
- 1 small-sized onion, chopped
- 1 garlic clove, minced
- 2 eggs, whisked
- 1 tsp baking powder
- 2 tbsp fresh cilantro, chopped
- Sea salt and ground black pepper, to taste
- 1 avocado, peeled, pitted and diced
- 2 tbsp sweet chili sauce

Directions

1. Preheat the air fryer to 370°F. In a mixing bowl, thoroughly combine the corn, onion, garlic, eggs, baking powder, cilantro, salt, and black pepper.
2. Shape the corn mixture into 6 patties and transfer them to the lightly greased air fryer basket.
3. Cook in the air fryer for 8 minutes; turn them over and cook for 7 minutes longer.
4. Serve the cakes with the avocado and chili sauce.

Nutrition: Calories: 383; Fats: 18.3 g; Carbohydrates: 42.8 g; Protein: 10.7 g

15
Blueberry Muffins

 10 minutes   10 minutes   10

Ingredients

- 1 cup almond flour
- 1 cup frozen blueberries
- 2 tsp baking powder
- 1 tsp olive oil
- ⅓ cup Erythritol sweetener
- 1 tsp vanilla extract, unsweetened
- ½ tsp salt & ¼ cup melted coconut oil
- 2 eggs, pastured
- ¼ cup applesauce, unsweetened
- ¼ cup almond milk, unsweetened

Directions

1. Switch on the air fryer, insert the fryer basket and grease it with olive oil. Next, set the fryer at 360°F, and preheat for 10 minutes.
2. Meanwhile, place flour in a large bowl, add blueberries, salt, sweetener, and baking powder, and stir until well combined.
3. Crack the eggs in another bowl. Whisk in vanilla, milk, and applesauce until combined, and then slowly whisk in the flour mixture until well combined.
4. Take 14 silicone muffin cups, grease them with oil, and then evenly fill them with the prepared batter.
5. Open the fryer; stack muffin cups inside and cook for 10 minutes until muffins are nicely golden brown and set.
6. When the air fryer beeps, transfer muffins onto a serving plate, and then make the remaining muffins in the same manner. Serve straight away.

Nutrition: Calories: 97; Carbohydrates: 6.3 g; Fats: 6.8 g; Protein: 3.3 g

16
Homemade Muffins

10 minutes

20 minutes

6

Ingredients

- 6 tbsp olive oil
- 1 tbsp Erythritol sweetener
- 2 eggs
- 100 g wholemeal flour
- 1 tsp baking powder
- Lemon zest

Directions

1. Using a whisk, beat the eggs with the sweetener. Add the oil, little by little, while stirring until you get a fluffy cream.
2. Then add the lemon zest.
3. Finally, sift the flour and the yeast into the previous mixture.
4. Fill ⅔ of the muffin baking tray with the dough.
5. Preheat the air fryer to 360°F for a few minutes and, when ready, place the muffins in the basket.
6. Cook until they are golden brown. This should take approximately 20 minutes.

Nutrition: Calories: 232; Carbohydrates: 28.3 g; Fats: 11.5 g; Protein: 4.0 g

Chapter 3
FISH RECIPES

17
Easy Tuna Wraps

 10 minutes 4 to 7 minutes 4

Ingredients

- 1 pound (454 g) fresh tuna steak, cut into 1-inch cubes
- 1 tbsp grated fresh ginger
- 2 garlic cloves, minced
- ½ tsp toasted sesame oil
- 4 low-sodium whole-wheat tortillas
- ¼ cup low-fat mayonnaise
- 2 cups shredded romaine lettuce
- 1 red bell pepper, thinly sliced

Directions

1. In a medium bowl, mix the tuna, ginger, garlic, and sesame oil. Let it stand for 10 minutes, then transfer it to the air fryer basket.
2. Air fry at 390°F for 4 to 7 minutes, or until done to your liking and lightly browned.
3. Make wraps with the tuna, tortillas, mayonnaise, lettuce, and bell pepper. Serve immediately.

Nutrition: Calories: 321; Carbohydrates: 21.8 g; Fats: 11.7 g; Protein: 31.5 g

18
Asian-Inspired Swordfish Steaks

 10 minutes 6 to 11 minutes 4

Ingredients

- 4 (4-oz / 113-g) swordfish steaks
- ½ tsp toasted sesame oil
- 1 jalapeño pepper, finely minced
- 2 garlic cloves, grated
- 1 tbsp grated fresh ginger
- ½ tsp Chinese five-spice powder
- ⅛ tsp freshly ground black pepper
- 2 tbsp freshly squeezed lemon juice

Directions

1. Place the swordfish steaks on a work surface and drizzle with the sesame oil.
2. In a small bowl, mix the jalapeño, garlic, ginger, five-spice powder, pepper, and lemon juice. Rub this mixture into the fish and let it stand for 10 minutes. Put in the air fryer basket.
3. Roast at 380°F for 6 to 11 minutes, or until the swordfish reaches an inner temperature of at least 140°F on a meat thermometer. Serve immediately.

Nutrition: Calories: 172; Carbohydrates: 1.8 g; Fats: 8.6 g; Protein: 22.3 g

19
Salmon with Fennel and Carrot

 15 minutes   13 to 14 minutes   2

Ingredients

- 1 fennel bulb, thinly sliced
- 1 large carrot, peeled and sliced
- 1 small onion, thinly sliced
- ¼ cup low-fat sour cream
- ¼ tsp coarsely ground pepper
- 2 (5-oz / 142-g) salmon fillets

Directions

1. Combine the fennel, carrot, and onion in a bowl and toss.
2. Put the vegetable mixture into a baking pan. Cook in the air fryer at 400°F for 4 minutes or until the vegetables are crisp-tender.
3. Remove the pan from the air fryer. Stir in the sour cream and sprinkle the vegetables with the pepper.
4. Top with the salmon fillets.
5. Return the pan to the air fryer. Roast for another 9 to 10 minutes or until the salmon just barely flakes when tested with a fork.

Nutrition: Calories: 359; Carbohydrates: 11.2 g; Fats: 21.5 g; Protein: 30.1 g

20
Ranch Tilapia fillets

 7 minutes   17 minutes   2 fillets

Ingredients

- 2 tbsp flour
- 1 egg, lightly beaten
- 1 cup crushed cornflakes
- 2 tbsp ranch seasoning
- 2 tilapia fillets
- Olive oil spray

Directions

1. Place a parchment liner in the air fryer basket.
2. Scoop the flour out onto a plate; set aside.
3. Put the beaten egg in a medium shallow bowl.
4. Put the cornflakes into a zip-top bag and crush them with a rolling pin or another small, blunt object.
5. On another plate, mix the crushed cereal and ranch seasoning.
6. Coat the tilapia fillets in the flour, dip them in the egg and then press them into the cornflake mixture.
7. Place the prepared fillets onto the liner in the air fryer in a single layer.
8. Spray lightly with olive oil, and air fry at 400°F for 8 minutes. Carefully flip the fillets and spray with more oil. Air fry for an additional 9 minutes, until golden and crispy, and serve.

Nutrition: Calories: 364; Carbohydrates: 26.2 g; Fats: 13.7 g; Protein: 33.4 g

21
Asian Sesame Cod

5 minutes | **7 to 9 minutes** | **1**

Ingredients

- 1 tbsp reduced-sodium soy sauce
- 2 tsp maple syrup
- 1 tsp sesame seeds
- 6 oz (170 g) cod fillet

Directions

1. In a small bowl, mix the soy sauce and maple syrup.
2. Spray the air fryer basket with nonstick cooking spray, then place the cod in the basket, brush with the soy mixture, and sprinkle sesame seeds on top. Roast at 360°F for 7 to 9 minutes or until opaque.
3. Remove the fryer's fish and allow to cool on a wire rack for 5 minutes before serving.

Nutrition: Calories: 299; Carbohydrates: 11.7 g; Fats: 13.1 g; Protein: 33.7 g

22
Lemon Scallops with Asparagus

10 minutes | **7 to 10 minutes** | **4**

Ingredients

- ½ pound (227 g) asparagus, ends trimmed and cut into 2-inch pieces
- 1 cup sugar snap peas
- 1 pound (454 g) sea scallops
- 1 tbsp lemon juice
- 2 tsp olive oil
- ½ tsp dried thyme
- Pinch salt
- Freshly ground black pepper, to taste

Directions

1. Put the asparagus and sugar snap peas in the air fryer basket. Air fry at 400°F for 2 to 3 minutes or until the vegetables start to feel tender.
2. Meanwhile, check the scallops for a small muscle attached to the side, pull it off and discard it.
3. In a medium-sized bowl, toss the scallops with lemon juice, olive oil, thyme, salt, and pepper. Place in the air fryer basket on top of the vegetables.
4. Air fry for 5 to 7 minutes, tossing the basket once during the cooking time. When the scallops are just firm when tested with your finger and opaque in the center, serve immediately.

Nutrition: Calories: 227; Carbohydrates: 8.3 g; Fats: 9.5 g; Protein: 27.3 g

23
Chilean Sea Bass with Green Olive Relish

 10 minutes   10 minutes   4

Ingredients

- Olive oil spray
- 2 (6-oz / 170-g) Chilean sea bass fillets or other firm-fleshed white fish
- 3 tbsp extra-virgin olive oil
- ½ tsp ground cumin
- ½ tsp salt
- ½ tsp black pepper
- ⅓ cup pitted green olives, diced
- ¼ cup finely diced onion
- 1 tsp chopped capers

Directions

1. Spray the air fryer basket with the olive oil spray. Drizzle the fillets with olive oil and sprinkle with the cumin, salt, and pepper. Put the fish in the air fryer basket. Bake at 325°F for 10 minutes, or until the fish flakes easily with a fork.
2. In the meantime, in a smaller bowl, stir together the olives, onion, and capers.
3. Serve the fish topped with the caper relish.

Nutrition: Calories: 204; Carbohydrates: 2.0 g; Fats: 12.8 g; Protein: 20.3 g

24
Ginger and Green Onion Fish

 15 minutes   15 minutes   2

Ingredients

BEAN SAUCE:
- 2 tbsp low-sodium soy sauce
- 1 tbsp rice wine
- 1 tbsp doubanjiang (Chinese black bean paste)
- 1 tsp minced fresh ginger
- 1 clove garlic, minced

VEGETABLES AND FISH:
- 1 tbsp peanut oil
- ¼ cup julienned green onions
- ¼ cup chopped fresh cilantro
- 2 tbsp julienned fresh ginger
- 2 (6-oz / 170-g) white fish fillets, such as tilapia

Directions

FOR THE SAUCE:
1. In a small bowl, mix all the ingredients and stir until well combined; set aside.

FOR THE VEGETABLES AND FISH:
1. In a medium bowl, combine the peanut oil, green onions, cilantro, and ginger. Toss to combine.
2. Cut 2 squares of parchment large enough to hold one fillet and half of the vegetables. Place one fillet on each parchment square, top with the vegetables, and the sauce over the top.
3. Fold the parchment paper over. Tuck the sides in tightly to hold the fish, vegetables, and sauce securely inside the packet.
4. Put the packets in a single layer in the air fryer basket. Roast at 350°F for 15 minutes.
5. Transfer each packet to a dinner plate. Cut open with scissors just before serving.

Nutrition: Calories: 361; Carbohydrates: 7.3 g; Fats: 17.9 g; Protein: 41.1 g

25
Fish Tacos

 15 minutes 9 to 12 minutes 4

Ingredients

- 1 pound (454 g) white fish fillets, such as snapper
- 1 tbsp olive oil
- 3 tbsp freshly squeezed lemon juice, divided
- 1 ½ cup chopped red cabbage
- ½ cup salsa
- ⅓ cup sour cream
- 4 whole-wheat tortillas
- 2 avocados, peeled and chopped

Directions

1. Spray the fish with olive oil and sprinkle with 1 tbsp of lemon juice. Place in the air fryer basket and air fry at 400°F for 9 to 12 minutes or until the fish just flakes when tested with a fork.
2. Meanwhile, combine the remaining 2 tbsp of lemon juice, cabbage, salsa, and sour cream in a medium bowl.
3. As soon as the fish is cooked, remove it from the air fryer basket and break it into large pieces.
4. Let everyone assemble their own taco combining the fish, tortillas, cabbage mixture and avocados.

Nutrition: Calories: 395; Carbohydrates: 11.8 g; Fats: 26.2 g; Protein: 29.5 g

26
Spicy Cajun Shrimp

 7 minutes 10 to 13 minutes 2 cups

Ingredients

- ½ pound (227 g) shrimp, peeled and deveined
- 1 tbsp olive oil
- 1 tsp ground cayenne pepper
- ½ tsp Old Bay seasoning
- ½ tsp paprika
- ⅛ tsp salt
- Juice of half a lemon

Directions

1. In a large bowl, mix the shrimp, olive oil, cayenne pepper, Old Bay Seasoning, paprika, and salt; toss to combine.
2. Transfer to the air fryer basket and roast at 390°F for 10 to 13 minutes, until browned.
3. Sprinkle a bit of lemon juice over the shrimp before serving.

Nutrition: Calories: 189; Carbohydrates: 2.1 g; Fats: 10.7 g; Protein: 20.3 g

27
Quick Shrimp Scampi

 10 minutes   7 to 8 minutes   2

Ingredients

- 30 (1 pound / 454 g) uncooked large shrimp, peeled, deveined, and tails removed
- 2 tsp olive oil
- 1 garlic clove, thinly sliced
- Juice and zest of ½ lemon
- ⅛ tsp salt
- Pinch red pepper flakes (optional)
- 1 tbsp chopped fresh parsley

Directions

1. Spray a baking pan with nonstick cooking spray, then combine the shrimp, olive oil, sliced garlic, lemon juice and zest, salt, and red pepper flakes (if using) in the pan, tossing to coat. Place in the air fryer basket.
2. Roast at 360°F for 7 to 8 minutes or until firm and bright pink.
3. Remove the fried shrimp, place on a serving plate and sprinkle the parsley on top. Serve warm.

Nutrition: Calories: 335; Carbohydrates: 2.5 g; Fats: 14.5 g; Protein: 48.6 g

28
Fish and Vegetable Tacos

 15 minutes   9 to 12 minutes   4

Ingredients

- 1-pound white fish fillets, such as sole or cod
- 2 tsp olive oil
- 3 tbsp freshly squeezed lemon juice
- 1½ cups chopped red cabbage
- 1 large carrot, grated
- ½ cup low-sodium salsa
- ⅓ cup low-fat Greek yogurt
- 4 soft low-sodium whole-wheat tortillas

Directions

1. Rub the fish with olive oil and drizzle with 1 tbsp of lemon juice. Fry in the air fryer basket for 9 to 12 minutes, or till the fish just flakes when tested with a fork.
2. In the meantime, in a medium bowl, stir together the remaining 2 tbsp of lemon juice, the red cabbage, carrot, salsa, and yogurt.
3. As soon as the fish is cooked, remove it from the air fryer basket and break it up into large pieces.

Nutrition: Calories: 287; Carbohydrates: 9.7 g; Fats: 13.5 g; Protein: 31.8 g

29
Snapper with Fruit

 15 minutes 9 to 13 minutes 4

Ingredients

- 4 (4-oz) red snapper fillets
- 2 tsp olive oil
- 3 nectarines, halved and pitted
- 3 plums, halved and pitted
- 1 cup red grapes
- 1 tbsp freshly squeezed lemon juice
- 1 tbsp maple syrup
- ½ tsp dried thyme

Directions

1. Put the red snapper in the air fryer basket and drizzle with the olive oil. Air-fry for 4 minutes.
2. Remove the basket and add the nectarines and plums. Scatter the grapes over the top.
3. Drizzle with lemon juice and maple syrup and sprinkle with thyme.
4. Replace the basket in the air fryer and air-fry for 5 to 9 minutes more, or till the fish flakes when tested with a fork and the fruit is tender. Serve immediately.

Nutrition: Calories: 236; Carbohydrates: 15.8 g; Fats: 7.4 g; Protein: 26.1 g

30
Tuna and Fruit Kebabs

 15 minutes  8 to 12 minutes 4

Ingredients

- 1 pound tuna steaks, cut into 1-inch cubes
- ½ cup canned pineapple chunks, drained, juice reserved
- ½ cup large red grapes
- 1 tbsp maple syrup
- 2 tsp grated fresh ginger
- 1 tsp olive oil
- Pinch cayenne pepper

Directions

1. Thread the tuna, pineapple, and grapes on 8 bamboo or 4 metal skewers that fit in the air fryer.
2. In a small bowl, whisk the maple syrup, 1 tbsp of reserved pineapple juice, ginger, olive oil, and cayenne. Brush this mixture over the kebabs. Let them stand for 10 minutes.
3. Grill the kebabs for 8 to 12 minutes, or until the tuna reaches an internal temperature of at least 145°F on a meat thermometer, and the fruit is tender and glazed. Brush the kebabs once with the remaining sauce. Discard any remaining marinade. Serve immediately.

Nutrition: Calories: 248.5; Carbohydrates: 11.4 g; Fats: 10.2 g; Protein: 26.8 g

31
Stevia Lemon Snapper with Fruit

 15 minutes   9 to 13 minutes   4

Ingredients

- 4 (4-oz / 113-g) red snapper fillets
- 2 tsp olive oil
- 3 nectarines, halved and pitted
- 3 plums, halved and pitted
- 1 cup red grapes
- 1 tbsp freshly squeezed lemon juice
- 1 tbsp stevia
- ½ tsp dried thyme

Directions

1. Put the red snapper in the air fryer basket and drizzle with the olive oil. Air fry at 390°F for 4 minutes.
2. Remove the basket and add the nectarines and plums. Scatter the grapes over the top.
3. Drizzle with the lemon juice and stevia and sprinkle with the thyme.
4. Return the basket to the air fryer and air fry for 5 to 9 minutes more, or until the fish flakes when tested with a fork and the fruit is tender. Serve immediately.

Nutrition: Calories: 297; Carbohydrates: 18.9 g; Fats: 12.4 g; Protein: 28.1 g

32
Breaded Hake with Green Chili Pepper and Mayonnaise

 15 minutes   30 minutes   4

Ingredients

- 4 breaded hake fillets
- 8 tsp mayonnaise
- Green Mojito
- 8 tsp extra virgin olive oil

Directions

1. Brush the breaded hake fillets with extra virgin olive oil.
2. Prepare the air fryer and put the hake fillets in the basket. Cook at 360°F for 30 minutes.
3. Meanwhile, put 8 tsp of mayonnaise and 2 tsp of green mojito in a bowl.
4. Serve the breaded hake fillets with the green mojito mayonnaise.

Nutrition: Calories: 226; Carbohydrates: 1.4 g; Fats: 14.3 g; Protein: 22.3 g

Chapter 4
BEEF RECIPES

33
Roast Beef

5 minutes | **45 minutes** | **3**

Ingredients

- 3 ½ pounds of beef joint
- 2 tbsp olive oil
- 1 tbsp rosemary
- ½ tbsp garlic powder
- ½ tsp fresh coarsely ground black pepper

Directions

1. Pre-heat the air fryer to 360°F
2. Mix herbs and oil on a plate. Roll the beef in the blend on the plate to ensure that the beef's entire surface is covered.
3. Place the beef in the air fryer basket. Set the timer for 45 minutes for rare beef and 51 minutes for 'well done'. Check the beef with a meat thermometer to check that it is done to your liking.
4. Cook for extra 6-minute periods if you would like it cooked more. Bear in mind that the roast will continue to cook while it is relaxing.
5. Remove the roast from the air fryer and put it on a plate, covering with lightweight aluminum foil. Allow it to rest for 10 minutes before serving.

Nutrition: Calories: 337; Carbohydrates: 0.4 g; Fats: 24.1 g; Protein: 32.1 g

34
Beef Empanadas

10 minutes | **10 minutes** | **3**

Ingredients

- 8 empanada discs, defrosted
- 1 cup picadillo
- 1 egg white, blended
- 1 tsp water
- Cooking spray

Directions

1. Set the air fryer at 325°F.
2. Spray cooking spray on the basket.
3. Place 2 tbsps of picadillo in each disc space. Fold in half and secure using a fork. Do the same for all the dough.
4. Mix water and egg whites. Sprinkle over the top of the empanadas.
5. Place 3 of them in your air fryer and allow them to bake for 10 minutes. Set them aside and do the same for the remaining empanadas.

Nutrition: Calories: 268; Carbohydrates: 22.5 g; Fats: 14.5 g; Protein: 11.2 g

35
Flavored Rib Eye Steak

 10 minutes   20 minutes   4

Ingredients

- 1 pound rib eye steak
- Salt and black pepper to the taste
- 1 tbsp olive oil

FOR THE RUB:
- 3 tbsp sweet paprika
- 2 tbsp onion powder
- 2 tbsp garlic powder
- 1 tbsp brown sugar
- 2 tbsp oregano, dried
- 1 tbsp cumin, ground
- 1 tbsp rosemary, dried

Directions

1. In a bowl, mix paprika with onion and garlic powder, sugar, oregano, rosemary, salt, pepper, and cumin. Stir and rub steak with this mix.
2. Season steak with salt and pepper. Rub again with the oil, place in the air fryer and, for 20 minutes, fry at 400°F, flipping them halfway.
3. Move the steak to a cutting board, slice and serve with a side salad.
4. Enjoy!

Nutrition: Calories: 292; Carbohydrates: 3.7 g; Fats: 18.1 g; Protein: 29.4 g

36
Steak

5 minutes | **15 minutes** | **2**

Ingredients

- 1 Ribeye Steak or New York City Strip Steak
- Salt and Pepper
- Garlic Powder
- Paprika
- Unsalted butter or grass-fed butter for serving, optional

Directions

1. Leave the meat to sit in a bowl at room temperature.
2. Spray olive oil onto both sides of the steak.
3. Add salt and pepper to season.
4. Add the garlic powder and paprika to the mixture.
5. Set the temperature of the air fryer to 400°F.
6. Put steak in the air fryer and cook for 12 minutes flipping it halfway through.
7. Dot it with butter when ready, then serve.

Nutrition: Calories: 277; Fats: 19.7 g; Carbohydrates: 0 g; Protein: 25.5 g

37
Chinese Steak and Broccoli

45 minutes | **12 minutes** | **4**

Ingredients

- ¾-pound round steak, cut into strips
- 1-pound broccoli florets
- ⅓ cup oyster sauce
- 2 tsp sesame oil
- 1 tsp soy sauce
- 1 tsp brown sugar
- ⅓ cup sherry
- 1 tbsp olive oil
- 1 garlic clove, minced

Directions

1. In a bowl, mix sesame oil with oyster sauce, soy sauce, sherry, and sugar, and stir well.
2. Add beef, toss, and leave to one side for 30 minutes.
3. Transfer beef to a pan that fits your air fryer, add broccoli, garlic, and oil, and toss everything.
4. Cook at 380°F for 12 minutes.
5. Divide among plates and serve.
6. Enjoy!

Nutrition: Calories: 306; Carbohydrates: 6.4 g; Fats: 20.5 g; Protein: 24.2 g

38
Mustard Marinated Beef

10 minutes | **45 minutes** | **6**

Ingredients

- 6 bacon strips
- 2 tbsp unsalted butter or grass-fed butter
- 3 garlic cloves, minced
- Salt and black pepper to taste
- 1 tbsp horseradish
- 1 tbsp mustard
- A 3 pounds beef joint for roasting
- 1 ¾ cup beef stock
- ¾ cup red wine

Directions

1. In a bowl, mix butter with mustard, garlic, salt, pepper and horseradish.
2. Whisk and rub the beef with this mix.
3. Arrange bacon strips on a cutting board and place the beef on top. Fold bacon around the beef, transfer to your air fryer's basket and cook at 400°F for 15 minutes. Transfer to a pan that fits your fryer.
4. Add stock and wine to the beef. Introduce the pan to your air fryer and cook at 360°F for 30 minutes more.
5. Carve the beef, divide among plates, and serve with a side salad.
6. Enjoy!

Nutrition: Calories: 463; Carbohydrates: 2.3 g; Fats: 33.1 g; Protein: 37.4 g

39
Beef Korma Curry

10 minutes | **17-20 minutes** | **4**

Ingredients

- 1 pound (454 g) sirloin steak, sliced
- ½ cup yogurt
- 1 tbsp curry powder
- 1 tbsp olive oil
- 1 onion, chopped
- 2 cloves garlic, minced
- 1 tomato, diced
- ½ cup frozen baby peas, thawed

Directions

1. In a medium bowl, combine the steak, yogurt, and curry powder. Stir and set aside.
2. In a metal bowl, combine the olive oil, onion, and garlic. Bake at 350°F for 3 to 4 minutes or until crisp and tender.
3. Add the steak along with the yogurt and the diced tomato. Bake for 12 to 13 minutes or until the steak is almost tender.
4. Stir in the peas and bake for 2 to 3 minutes or until hot.

Nutrition: Calories: 313; Carbohydrates: 5.9 g; Fats: 19.1 g; Protein: 28.3 g

40
Low-fat Steak

 25 minutes   10 minutes   3

Ingredients

- 400 g beef steak
- 1 tsp white pepper
- 1 tsp turmeric
- 1 tsp cilantro
- 1 tsp olive oil
- 3 tsp lemon juice
- 1 tsp oregano
- 1 tsp salt
- 100 g water

Directions

1. Rub the steaks with white pepper and turmeric and put them in a large bowl.
2. Sprinkle the meat with salt, oregano, cilantro and lemon juice.
3. Leave the steak for 20 minutes.
4. Combine olive oil and water and pour it into the bowl with the steaks.
5. Cook the steaks in the air fryer for 10 minutes on both sides.
6. Serve it immediately.

Nutrition: Calories: 311; Carbohydrates: 1.4 g; Fats: 19.1 g; Protein: 31.7 g

41
Beef with Mushrooms

 15 minutes   40 minutes   4

Ingredients

- 300 g beef
- 150 g mushrooms
- 1 onion
- 1 tsp olive oil
- 100 g vegetable broth
- 1 tsp basil
- 1 tsp chili
- 30 g tomato juice

Directions

1. For this recipe, you should take a solid piece of beef. Take the beef and pierce the meat with a knife.
2. Rub it with olive oil, basil, chili and lemon juice.
3. Chop the onion and mushrooms.
4. Cook the vegetables in the vegetable broth for 5 minutes.
5. Take a big tray and put the meat in it. Add vegetable broth to the tray too. It will make the meat juicy.
6. Preheat the air fryer oven to 360°F and cook it for 35 minutes.

Nutrition: Calories: 232; Protein: 22.9 g; Fats: 12.2 g; Carbohydrates: 6.4 g

42
Beef Schnitzel

 5 minutes 15 minutes 1

Ingredients

- 1 lean beef schnitzel
- 1 tbsp olive oil
- ¼ cup breadcrumbs
- 1 egg
- 1 lemon, to serve

Directions

1. Heat the air fryer to 360°F.
2. In a big bowl, add breadcrumbs and oil, and mix well until it forms a crumbly mixture
3. Dip the beef steak in the whisked egg and coat in the breadcrumbs mixture.
4. Place the breaded beef in the air fryer and cook at 360°F for 15 minutes or more until fully cooked through.
5. Remove from the air fryer and serve with the side of salad greens and lemon.

Nutrition: Calories: 404; Protein: 32.1 g; Carbohydrates: 14.0 g; Fats: 23.7 g

43
Beef Steak Kabobs with Vegetables

 5 minutes 10 minutes 4

Ingredients

- 2 tbsp light soy sauce
- 4 cups lean beef chuck ribs, cut into one-inch pieces
- ⅓ cup low-fat sour cream
- ½ onion
- 8 (6-inch) skewers
- 1 bell peppers

Directions

1. Pre-heat the air fryer to 400°F.
2. In a mixing bowl, add soy sauce and sour cream, and mix well. Add the lean beef chunks, coat well, and let it marinate for half an hour or more.
3. Cut the onion and bell pepper into one-inch pieces. In water, soak skewers for ten minutes.
4. Add onions, bell peppers, and beef on skewers; alternatively, sprinkle with black pepper
5. Let it cook for 10 minutes and flip halfway through.
6. Serve with yogurt dipping sauce.

Nutrition: Calories: 237; Protein: 25.3 g; Carbohydrates: 4.8 g; Fats: 13.1 g

44
Beef Scallops

 9 minutes 27 minutes 4

Ingredients

- 16 veal scallops
- Salt
- Ground pepper
- Garlic powder
- 2 eggs
- Breadcrumbs
- Extra virgin olive oil

Directions

1. Pre-heat the air fryer to 360°F. Sprinkle the veal scallops with salt, and pepper. Add some garlic powder.
2. In a bowl, beat the eggs.
3. Put the breadcrumbs in a separate bowl.
4. Coat the beef scallops first in beaten egg and then in breadcrumbs.
5. Spray with extra virgin olive oil on both sides.
6. Put a batch of scallops (about 4 or 5) in the basket of the air fryer. Do not pile them too high.
7. Cook for 15 minutes. From time to time, shake the basket so that the scallops move.
8. Repeat the process with each batch of scallops.
9. Serve and enjoy!

Nutrition: Calories: 351; Fats: 23.4 g; Carbohydrates: 4.2 g; Protein: 28.9 g

Chapter 5
PORK RECIPES

45
Ranch Pork Chops

 10 minutes 12 minutes 4

Ingredients

- 4 pork chops
- 1 egg, lightly beaten
- 1 packet of ranch seasoning
- 2 cups breadcrumbs
- ½ cup of milk
- Pepper
- Salt

Directions

1. In a shallow bowl, whisk egg, milk, pepper, and salt.
2. In a shallow dish, mix together breadcrumbs and ranch seasoning.
3. Dip pork chops in egg and coat with breadcrumbs.
4. Place the dehydrating tray in a multi-level air fryer basket and place the basket in the inside.
5. Place the pork chops on the dehydrating tray.
6. Seal the pot with the air fryer lid. Select the air fry mode and then set the temperature to 360 °F and the timer for 12 minutes. Turn the pork chops halfway through.
7. Serve and enjoy.

Nutrition: Calories: 357; Fats: 17.8 g; Carbohydrates: 19.5 g; Protein: 29.6 g

46
Glazed Pork Shoulder

 15 minutes 18 minutes 5

Ingredients

- ⅓ cup soy sauce
- 2 tbsp brown sugar
- 1 tbsp stevia
- 2 pounds pork shoulder, cut into 1½-inch thick slices

Directions

1. In a bowl, mix together all the soy sauce, sugar, and stevia.
2. Add the pork and generously coat with the marinade.
3. Cover and refrigerate to marinate for about 4-6 hours.
4. Set the temperature of the air fryer to 335°F. Grease an air fryer basket.
5. Place the pork shoulder in the prepared air fryer basket.
6. Air fry for about 10 minutes and then another 6-8 minutes at 390 °F.
7. Remove from the air fryer and transfer the pork shoulder onto a platter.
8. Cover the pork with a piece of foil for about 10 minutes before serving.
9. Enjoy!

Nutrition: Calories: 465; Carbohydrates: 7.8 g; Protein: 39.1 g; Fats: 30.4 g

47
Pork Shoulder with Pineapple Sauce

 20 minutes 24 minutes 3

Ingredients

FOR PORK:
- 10 ½ oz pork shoulder, cut into bite-sized pieces
- 2 pinches seasoning
- 1 tsp light soy sauce
- A dash of sesame oil
- 1 egg
- ¼ cup plain flour

FOR SAUCE:
- 1 tsp olive oil
- 1 medium onion, sliced
- 1 tbsp garlic, minced
- 1 large pineapple slice, cubed
- 1 medium tomato, chopped
- 2 tbsp tomato sauce
- 2 tbsp oyster sauce
- 1 tbsp Worcestershire sauce
- 1 tsp sugar
- 1 tbsp water
- ½ tbsp corn flour

Directions

FOR THE PORK:
1. In a large bowl, mix together the seasoning, soy sauce, and sesame oil.
2. Add the pork cubes and generously mix with the mixture.
3. Refrigerate to marinate for about 4-6 hours.
4. In a shallow dish, beat the egg.
5. In another dish, place the plain flour.
6. Dip the cubed pork in the beaten egg and then coat evenly with the flour.
7. Set the temperature of the air fryer to 248°F. Grease an air fryer basket.
8. Arrange the pork cubes into the prepared air fryer basket in a single layer.
9. Air fry for about 20 minutes.

MEANWHILE, FOR THE SAUCE:
1. In a skillet, heat oil over a medium heat and sauté the onion and garlic for about 1 minute.
2. Add the pineapple and tomato and cook for about 1 minute.
3. Add the tomato sauce, oyster sauce, Worcestershire sauce, and sugar and stir to combine.
4. Meanwhile, in a bowl, mix together the water and corn flour.
5. Add the corn flour mixture into the sauce, stirring continuously.
6. Cook until the sauce is thickened enough, stirring continuously.
7. Remove the pork cubes from the air fryer and add them to the sauce.
8. Cook for about 1-2 minutes or until completely coated.
9. Remove from the heat and serve hot.

Note: If you don't have fresh pineapple to hand, use canned pineapple. However, remember to leave out sugar from the sauce.

Nutrition: Calories: 445; Carbohydrates: 37.5 g; Protein: 24.8 g; Fats: 23.1 g

48
Bacon Wrapped Pork Tenderloin

 15 minutes   30 minutes   4

Ingredients

- 1 ½-pound pork tenderloins
- 4 bacon strips
- 2 tbsp Dijon mustard

Directions

1. Coat the tenderloin evenly with mustard.
2. Wrap the tenderloin with bacon strips.
3. Set the temperature of the air fryer to 360°F. Grease an air fryer basket.
4. Arrange the pork tenderloin in the prepared air fryer basket.
5. Air fry for about 15 minutes.
6. Flip and air fry for another 10-15 minutes.
7. Remove from the air fryer and transfer the pork tenderloin to a platter. Wait for about 5 minutes before slicing.
8. Slice the tenderloin to the thickness that you prefer and serve.

Nutrition: Calories: 477; Carbohydrates: 1.2 g; Protein: 54.2 g; Fats: 28.4 g

49
Pork Tenderloin with Bell Peppers

  20 minutes   15 minutes   3

Ingredients

- 1 big red bell pepper, seeded and cut into thin strips
- 1 red onion, thinly sliced
- 2 tsp herbs de Provence
- Salt and ground black pepper, as required
- 1 tbsp olive oil
- 10 ½ oz pork tenderloin, cut into 4 pieces
- ½ tbsp Dijon mustard

Directions

1. In a bowl, add the bell pepper, onion, herbs de Provence, salt, black pepper, and ½ tbsp of oil and toss to coat well.
2. Rub the pork pieces with mustard, salt, and black pepper.
3. Drizzle with the remaining oil.
4. Set the temperature of the air fryer to 390°F. Grease an air fryer pan.
5. Place the bell pepper mixture into the prepared air fryer pan and top with the pork pieces.
6. Air fry for about 15 minutes, flipping once halfway through.
7. Remove from the air fryer and transfer the pork mixture onto serving plates.
8. Serve hot.

Nutrition: Calories: 218; Carbohydrates: 7.1 g; Protein: 27.7 g; Fats: 8.8 g

50
Pork Loin with Potatoes

15 minutes | 25 minutes | 5

Ingredients

- 2 pounds pork loin
- 3 tbsp olive oil, divided
- 1 tsp fresh parsley, chopped
- Salt and ground black pepper, as required
- 3 large red potatoes, chopped
- ½ tsp garlic powder
- ½ tsp red pepper flakes, crushed

Directions

1. Coat the pork loin with oil and then season evenly with parsley, salt, and black pepper.
2. In a large bowl, mix the potatoes, remaining oil, garlic powder, red pepper flakes, salt, and black pepper and toss to coat well.
3. Set the temperature of the air fryer to 325°F. Grease an air fryer basket.
4. Place the loin into the prepared air fryer basket.
5. Arrange potato pieces around the pork loin.
6. Air fry for about 25 minutes.
7. Remove from the air fryer and transfer the pork loin onto a platter.
8. Wait for about 5 minutes before slicing.
9. Cut the pork loin into slices and serve alongside the potatoes.

Nutrition: Calories: 482; Carbohydrates: 23.6 g; Protein: 37.9 g; Fats: 26.3 g

51
Pork Spare Ribs

15 minutes | 20 minutes | 4

Ingredients

- 5-6 garlic cloves, minced
- ½ cup rice vinegar
- 2 tbsp soy sauce
- Salt and ground black pepper, as required
- 12 (1-inch) pork spare ribs
- ½ cup cornstarch
- 2 tbsp olive oil

Directions

1. In an large bowl, mix the garlic, vinegar, soy sauce, salt, and black pepper.
2. Add the ribs and generously coat with the mixture.
3. Refrigerate to marinate overnight.
4. Put the cornstarch in a shallow bowl.
5. Coat the ribs evenly with cornstarch and then drizzle with oil.
6. Set the temperature of the air fryer to 390°F. Grease an air fryer basket.
7. Arrange the ribs in the prepared air fryer basket in a single layer.
8. Air fry for about 10 minutes per side.
9. Remove from the air fryer and transfer the ribs onto serving plates.
10. Serve immediately.

Nutrition: Calories: 264; Carbohydrates: 14.5 g; Protein: 15.1 g; Fats: 16.3 g

52
BBQ Pork Ribs

 15 minutes 26 minutes 4

Ingredients

- ¼ cup stevia, divided
- ¾ cup BBQ sauce
- 2 tbsp tomato ketchup
- 1 tbsp Worcestershire sauce*
- 1 tbsp soy sauce
- ½ tsp garlic powder
- Freshly ground white pepper to taste
- 1 ¾ pound pork ribs

Directions

1. In a basin, mix 3 tbsp of stevia and the remaining ingredients except for the pork ribs.
2. Add the pork ribs and generously coat with the mixture.
3. Refrigerate to marinate for about 20 minutes.
4. Set the temperature of the air fryer to 355°F. Grease an air fryer basket.
5. Arrange the ribs in the prepared air fryer basket in a single layer.
6. Air fry for about 13 minutes per side.
7. Remove from the air fryer and transfer the ribs onto plates.
8. Drizzle with the remaining stevia and serve immediately.

Note: Worcestershire sauce* - The other ingredients that make up this savory sauce usually include onions, molasses, high fructose corn syrup: depending on the country of production, salt, garlic, tamarind, cloves, chili pepper extract, water and natural flavorings.

Nutrition: Calories: 454; Carbohydrates: 13.7 g; Protein: 23.1 g; Fats: 32.3 g

53
Pork Fillets with Serrano Ham

 10 minutes 20 minutes 4

Ingredients

- 400 g very thinly sliced pork fillets
- 2 boiled and chopped eggs
- 100 g chopped Serrano ham
- 1 beaten egg
- Breadcrumbs

Directions

1. Roll the eggs and ham up in the pork fillets. So that the rolls do not lose their shape, fasten with a string or kebab sticks.
2. Pass the rolls through the beaten egg and then through the breadcrumbs until they are covered in a good layer.
3. Set the temperature of the air fryer to 360°F.
4. Put the rolls into the air fryer basket and cook them for 8 minutes.
5. Serve.

Nutrition: Calories: 335; Fats: 17.1 g; Carbohydrates: 10.8 g; Protein: 34.4 g

54
Pork in a Blanket

 5 minutes 10 minutes 4

Ingredients

- ½ defrosted puff pastry sheet
- 16 thick smoked sausages
- 15 ml milk

Directions

1. Prepare the air fryer and set it to 390°F. Set the timer to 5 minutes.
2. Cut the puff pastry into 64 x 38 mm strips.
3. Place a cocktail sausage at the end of the puff pastry and roll the sausage inside, finally sealing the dough with some water.
4. Brush the tops of the wrapped sausages with milk and place them in the preheated air fryer.
5. Cook for 10 minutes until golden brown.

Nutrition: Calories: 435; Fats: 33.4 g; Carbohydrates: 11.8 g; Protein: 22.3 g

55
Provencal Ribs

 10 minutes 1 hour and 20 minutes 4

Ingredients

- 500 g pork ribs
- Provencal herbs
- Salt
- Ground pepper
- ½ tsp oil

Directions

1. Prepare the ribs in a bowl and add some oil, Provencal herbs, salt, and ground pepper.
2. Stir well and leave in the fridge for at least 1 hour.
3. Pre-heat the air-fryer to 400°F.
4. Put the ribs in the basket and cook for 20 minutes.
5. From time to time, shake the basket and remove the ribs.

Nutrition: Calories: 354; Fats: 28.6 g; Carbohydrates: 1.1 g; Protein: 24.7 g

56
Marinated Loin Potatoes

Ingredients

- 2 medium potatoes
- 4 fillets of marinated pork loin
- A little extra virgin olive oil
- Salt to taste

Directions

1. Peel the potatoes and slice them with a match-sized mandolin.
2. Wash and immerse in water for 30 minutes. Drain and dry well.
3. Place them in bowl and add a little oil. Stir so that the oil permeates well into all the potatoes.
4. Spread them in the base of the air fryer basket, distributing them evenly.
5. Cook at 325°F for 10 minutes.
6. Take out the basket, and shake. Check that the potatoes are tender. If not, cook for 5 more minutes.
7. Arrange the steaks on top of the potatoes.
8. Turn up the air fryer to 360°F.
9. Cook for 10 minutes. Check and then add 5 minutes more if necessary.
10. Serve and enjoy.

Nutrition: Calories: 374; Fats: 15.5 g; Carbohydrates: 31.9 g; Protein: 26.7 g

57
Pork Bondiola Chop

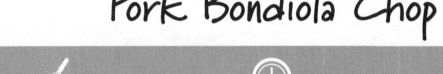

Ingredients

- 1 kg bondiola in pieces
- Breadcrumbs
- 2 beaten eggs
- Seasoning to taste

Directions

1. Cut the bondiola into small pieces
2. Add seasoning to taste.
3. Pour the beaten eggs onto the seasoned bondiola.
4. Add the breadcrumbs.
5. Cook in the air fryer for 20 minutes while turning the food halfway.
6. Serve

Nutrition: Calories: 366; Fats: 23.3 g; Carbohydrates: 11.7 g; Protein: 27.1 g

58
Pork Tenderloin

 10 minutes 20 minutes 6

Ingredients

- ½ pound pork tenderloin patted dry
- Non-stick cooking spray
- 2 tbsps. garlic scape pesto
- Salt
- Pepper

Directions

1. Set the air fryer temperature to 375°F.
2. Massage all sides of the tenderloin with the non-stick cooking spray
3. Add pepper, garlic scape pesto, and salt.
4. Sprinkle the air fryer basket with cooking spray.
5. Place the tenderloin on the air fryer basket.
6. Cook for 10 minutes.
7. Turn and cook for another 10 minutes on the second side.
8. Remove from the air fryer.
9. Serve

Nutrition: Calories: 119; Protein: 11.4 g; Fats: 8.2 g; Carbohydrates: 0.5 g

59
Roast Pork

 10 minutes 50 minutes 6

Ingredients

- 2 pounds pork loin
- 1 tbsp olive oil
- 1 tsp salt

Directions

1. Set the temperature of the air fryer to 360°F.
2. Apply the oil to the pork.
3. Add salt.
4. Cook the pork in the air fryer for about 50 minutes. Shake halfway through the cooking.
5. Remove the pork from the air fryer and allow it to cool.
6. Serve.

Nutrition: Calories: 368; Fats: 25.5 g; Carbohydrates: 0 g; Protein: 33.1 g

60
Fried Pork Chops

 5 minutes 35 minutes 2

Ingredients

- 3 cloves of garlic, minced
- 2 tbsp olive oil
- 1 tbsp marinade
- 2 thawed pork chops

Directions

1. In a bowl, mix the garlic, oil, and marinade.
2. Apply the mixture to the pork chops.
3. Put the chops in the air fryer and cook at 360°C for 35 minutes.

Nutrition: Calories: 368; Fats: 26.8 g; Carbohydrates: 2.0 g; Protein: 26.1 g

61
Creamy Pork

 10 minutes 22 minutes 6

Ingredients

- 2 pounds of pork meat, boneless and cubed
- 2 yellow onions, chopped
- 1 tbsp of olive oil
- 1 garlic clove, minced
- 3 cups of chicken stock
- 2 tbsp of sweet paprika
- Salt and black pepper to the taste
- 2 tbsp white flour
- 1 ½ cups sour cream
- 2 tbsp dill, chopped

Directions

1. Using a pan for the air fryer, mix pepper, salt and oil with the pork and rub well.
2. Put them all in the air fryer and cook at 360°F for 7 minutes.
3. Add onion, garlic, stock, paprika, flour, sour cream, and dill. Toss and cook at 370°F for 15 minutes more.
4. Divide everything onto plates and serve right away.
5. Enjoy!

Nutrition: Calories: 413; Fats: 28.4 g; Carbohydrates: 5.2 g; Protein: 34.2 g

62
Mesquite Pork Chops

 10 minutes   14 minutes   2

Ingredients

- 2 pork chops
- 1 tbsp olive oil
- 2 tbsp stevia
- 1 ½ tbsp mesquite seasoning
- Pepper
- Salt

Directions

1. Mix together oil, stevia, mesquite seasoning, pepper and salt and rub these all over the pork chops.
2. Place the dehydrating tray in a multi-level air fryer basket and place the basket in the air fryer.
3. Place the pork chops on the dehydrating tray.
4. Seal the pot with the air fryer lid and select air fry mode. Then, set the temperature to 380°F and cook for 14 minutes. Turn the pork chops halfway through.
5. Serve and enjoy.

Nutrition: Calories: 218; Carbohydrates: 1.1 g; Fats: 14.1 g; Protein: 21.4 g

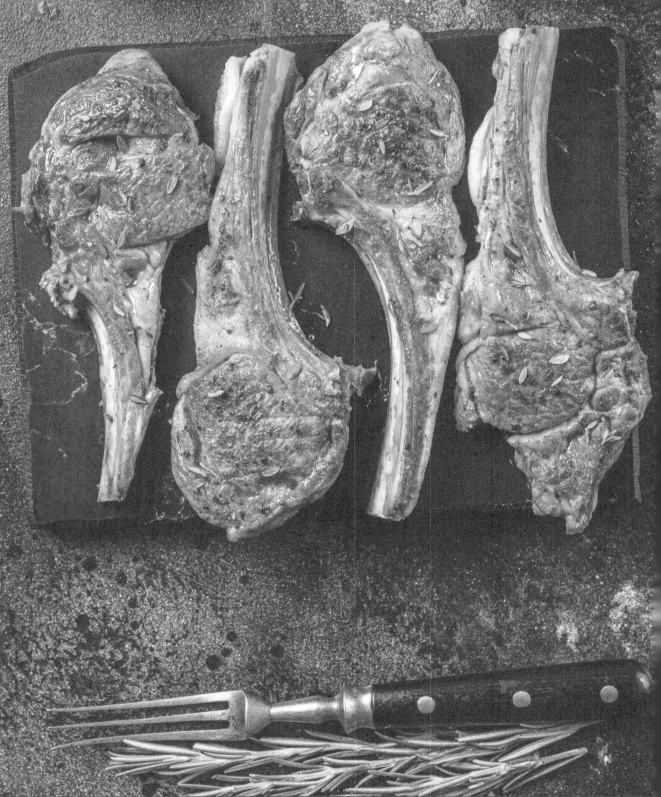

Chapter 6
LAMB RECIPES

63
Juicy Lamb Chops

 10 minutes 14 minutes 4

Ingredients

- 4 lamb chops
- 2 garlic cloves, minced
- 2 tbsp olive oil
- Pepper
- Salt

Directions

1. Coat lamb chops with oil and rub with garlic, pepper, and salt.
2. Place the dehydrating tray in a multi-level air fryer basket and place the basket in the air fryer.
3. Place lamb chops on the dehydrating tray.
4. Close the air fryer lid and select air fry mode. Then, set the temperature to 350°F and cook for 14 minutes. Turn the lamb chops halfway through.
5. Serve and enjoy.

Nutrition: Calories: 294; Fats: 23.1 g; Carbohydrates: 0 g; Protein: 21.8 g

64
Crispy Lamb

 10 minutes 30 minutes 4

Ingredients

- 1 tbsp breadcrumbs
- 2 tbsp macadamia nuts, toasted and crushed
- 1 tbsp olive oil
- 1 garlic clove, minced
- 28 oz rack of lamb
- Salt and black pepper to the taste
- 1 egg
- 1 tbsp rosemary, chopped

Directions

1. In a bowl, mix oil with garlic and stir well.
2. Season the lamb with the salt and pepper and brush with the oil.
3. In another bowl, mix the nuts with the breadcrumbs and rosemary.
4. Break an egg into a separate bowl. Whisk well.
5. Dip the lamb in the egg, then in the macadamia mix. Place them in your air fryer's basket. Cook at 360°F and cook for 25 minutes.
6. Increase the heat to 400°F and cook for 5 minutes more.
7. Divide among plates and serve right away.
8. Enjoy!

Nutrition: Calories: 313; Fats: 22.8 g; Carbohydrates: 2.6 g; Protein: 24.2 g

65
Lamb and Creamy Brussels Sprouts

 10 minutes    1 hour and 10 minutes   4

Ingredients

- 2 pounds leg of lamb, scored
- 2 tbsp olive oil
- 1 tbsp rosemary, chopped
- 1 tbsp lemon thyme, chopped
- 1 garlic clove, minced
- 1 ½ pound Brussels sprouts, trimmed
- 1 tbsp unsalted butter or grass-fed butter
- ½ cup sour cream
- Salt and black pepper to the taste

Directions

1. Season the leg of lamb with salt, pepper, thyme and rosemary.
2. Brush with oil, place in your air fryer's basket and cook at 300°F for 1 hour. Then, transfer to a plate to keep warm.
3. Using an air fryer pan, mix Brussels sprouts with salt, pepper, garlic, butter and sour cream. Toss them and put them in your air fryer. Cook at 400°F for 10 minutes.
4. Divide the lamb on plates, add Brussels sprouts on the side and serve.
5. Enjoy!

Nutrition: Calories: 499; Fats: 38.8 g; Carbohydrates: 6.2 g; Protein: 30.8 g

66
Rosemary Lamb Chops

 30 minutes   20 minutes   2 to 3

Ingredients

- 2 tsp oil
- ½ tsp ground rosemary
- ½ tsp lemon juice
- 1 pound (454 g) lamb chops, approximately 1-inch thick
- Salt and pepper to taste
- Cooking spray

Directions

1. Mix the oil, rosemary, and lemon juice and rub them into all sides of the lamb chops. Season with salt and pepper to taste.
2. For the best flavor, cover lamb chops and allow them to rest in the fridge for 15 to 20 minutes.
3. Spray the air fryer basket with nonstick spray and place the lamb chops inside.
4. Air fry at 360°F for approximately 20 minutes. This will cook the chops to 'medium'. The meat will be juicy but have no remaining pink. Air fry for 1 to 2 minutes longer for well-done chops. For rare chops, stop cooking after about 12 minutes and check.

Nutrition: Calories: 405; Fats: 29.6 g; Protein: 33.4 g; Carbohydrates: 1.2 g

67
Za'atar Lamb Loin Chops

 10 minutes
 15-20 minutes
 4

Ingredients

- 8 (3 ½-oz) bone-in lamb loin chops, trimmed
- 3 garlic cloves, crushed
- 1 tbsp fresh lemon juice
- 1 tsp olive oil
- 1 tbsp za'atar
- Salt and black pepper, to taste

Directions

1. Preheat the air fryer to 400°F and grease an air fryer basket.
2. Mix the garlic, lemon juice, oil, za'atar, salt, and black pepper in a large bowl.
3. Coat the chops generously with the herb mixture and arrange the chops in the air fryer basket.
4. Cook for about 15 minutes, flipping twice in between, and dish out the lamb chops to serve hot.

Nutrition: Calories: 404; Fats: 29.6 g; Carbohydrates: 0.6 g; Protein: 34.1 g

68
Spiced Lamb Steaks

 15 minutes
 15 minutes
 3

Ingredients

- ½ onion, roughly chopped
- 1 ½ pounds boneless lamb sirloin steaks
- 5 garlic cloves, peeled
- 1 tbsp fresh ginger, peeled
- 1 tsp garam masala
- 1 tsp ground fennel
- ½ tsp ground cumin
- ½ tsp ground cinnamon
- ½ tsp cayenne pepper
- Salt and black pepper, to taste

Directions

1. Preheat the air fryer to 330°F and grease an air fryer basket.
2. Put the onion, garlic, ginger, and spices in a blender and pulse until smooth.
3. Coat the lamb steaks with this mixture on both sides and refrigerate to marinate for about 24 hours.
4. Arrange the lamb steaks in the air fryer basket and cook for about 15 minutes, flipping once in between.
5. Dish out the steaks on a platter and serve warm.

Nutrition: Calories: 430; Fats: 27.7 g; Carbohydrates: 4.2 g; Protein: 39.7 g

Chapter 7
POULTRY RECIPES

69
Soy Chicken and Sesame

 10 minutes 50 minutes 4

Ingredients

- 1 large chicken breast
- 2 eggs
- ½ cup breadcrumbs
- ½ tsp extra virgin olive oil
- ¼ tbsp salt
- Ground pepper, to taste
- ½ cup soy sauce
- ¼ cup sesame

Directions

1. Cut the breast into fillets and put them in a bowl.
2. Season the chicken.
3. Add soy sauce and sesame. Mix well and leave for 30 minutes.
4. Beat the eggs. Cover all the steaks with the beaten egg and the breadcrumbs.
5. With a silicone brush, brush the fillets with the oil on both sides.
6. Place on the grill of the air fryer and select 360°F.
7. Make the fillets in batches. Grill for 20 minutes.

Nutrition: Calories: 192; Carbohydrates: 10.2 g; Fats: 9.3 g; Protein: 16.8 g

70
Chicken Fajitas with Avocados

 10 minutes 10 to 14 minutes 4

Ingredients

- 4 boneless, skinless chicken breasts, sliced
- 1 small red onion, sliced
- 2 red bell peppers, sliced
- ½ cup spicy ranch salad dressing, divided
- ½ tsp dried oregano
- 8 corn tortillas
- 2 cups torn butter lettuce
- 2 avocados, peeled and chopped

Directions

1. Place the chicken, onion, and pepper in the air fryer basket. Drizzle with 1 tbsp of the salad dressing and add the oregano. Toss to combine.
2. Air fry at 380°F for 10 to 14 minutes or until the chicken is 165°F on a food thermometer.
3. Transfer the chicken and vegetables to a bowl and toss with the remaining salad dressing.
4. Serve the chicken mixture with the tortillas, lettuce, and avocados, and let everyone make their own creations.

Nutrition: Calories: 316; Carbohydrates: 16.8 g; Fats: 16.3 g; Protein: 25.8 g

71
Herbed Chicken Marsala

 10 minutes 30 minutes 4

Ingredients

- salt and freshly ground black pepper
- 4-oz boneless, skinless chicken breast cutlets
- ¾ cup low-sodium chicken broth
- 2 tsp unsalted butter
- 2 tbsp fresh flat-leaf parsley, roughly chopped
- 10 oz white button or cremini (Baby Bella) mushrooms, sliced
- ⅓ cup whole wheat flour
- ⅓ cup sweet marsala wine
- ⅓ cup sun-dried tomatoes (not packed in oil; not rehydrated), finely chopped or very thinly sliced
- ½ tsp chopped fresh rosemary
- 1 ½ tbsp extra-virgin olive oil

Directions

1. Pound the chicken cutlets to flatten them. Sprinkle with ¼ tsp each of salt and pepper.
2. Coat the chicken with flour and air fry for about 4 minutes. It should be golden brown by then. Place it in an airtight container to keep it warm.
3. After removing the chicken, add rosemary, sun-dried tomatoes and ½ a cup of the chicken broth to what is left in the fryer after the chicken is removed. Cook the mixture for a minute.
4. Mix the mushrooms with ½ tsp of pepper and ¼ tsp of salt. Cook the mixture for 5 minutes to make the mushrooms soft.
5. Add marsala to the mushroom mixture and simmer them together.
6. Add the remaining ¼ cup of broth to the butter and cook them with low heat to melt the butter. This should not exceed 30 seconds.
7. Top the chicken with the sauce and mushroom mixture before you serve it. You should also sprinkle it with some parsley.

Nutrition: Calories: 288; Carbohydrates: 17.9 g; Fats: 11.2 g; Protein: 29.3 g

72
Greek Chicken Kebabs

 15 minutes 15 minutes 4

Ingredients

- 3 tbsp freshly squeezed lemon juice
- 2 tsp olive oil
- 2 tbsp chopped fresh flat-leaf parsley
- ½ tsp dried oregano
- ½ tsp dried mint
- 1 pound (454 g) low-sodium boneless, skinless chicken breasts, cut into 1-inch pieces
- 1 cup cherry tomatoes
- 1 small yellow summer squash, cut into 1-inch cubes

Directions

1. In a large bowl, whisk the lemon juice, olive oil, parsley, oregano, and mint.
2. Add the chicken and stir to coat. Let the mixture stand for 10 minutes at room temperature.
3. Alternating the items, thread the chicken, tomatoes, and squash onto 8 bamboo or metal skewers that fit in an air fryer. Brush with marinade.
4. Air fry the kebabs at 380°F for about 15 minutes, brushing once with any remaining marinade, until the chicken reaches an internal temperature of 165°F on a meat thermometer. Discard any remaining marinade. Serve immediately.

Nutrition: Calories: 206; Carbohydrates: 9.8 g; Fats: 6.4 g; Protein: 27.8 g

73
Stevia Lemon Garlic Chicken

 10 minutes   16 to 19 minutes   4

Ingredients

- 4 (5-oz / 142-g) low-sodium boneless, skinless chicken breasts, cut into 4-by-½-inch strips
- 2 tsp olive oil
- 2 tbsp cornstarch
- 3 garlic cloves, minced
- ½ cup low-sodium chicken broth
- ¼ cup freshly squeezed lemon juice
- 1 tbsp stevia
- ½ tsp dried thyme
- Brown rice, cooked (optional)

Directions

1. In a large bowl, mix the chicken and olive oil. Sprinkle with the cornstarch. Toss to coat.
2. Add the garlic and transfer to a baking pan. Bake in the air fryer at 400°F for 10 minutes, stirring once during cooking.
3. Add the chicken broth, lemon juice, stevia, and thyme to the chicken mixture. Bake for 6 to 9 minutes more, or until the sauce is slightly thickened and the chicken reaches an internal temperature of 165°F on a meat thermometer. Serve over hot cooked brown rice, if desired.

Nutrition: Calories: 230; Carbohydrates: 6.6 g; Fats: 8.3 g; Protein: 32.3 g

74
Chicken with Provencal Herbs and Potatoes

 10 minutes   55 minutes   2

Ingredients

- 4 potatoes
- 2 chicken hindquarters
- Provencal herbs
- Salt to taste
- ¼ tsp ground pepper, or to taste
- ½ tsp extra virgin olive oil

Directions

1. Peel the potatoes and cut them into slices.
2. Sprinkle with pepper and put on the grid of the air fryer base.
3. Smother the chicken well with oil, salt and pepper. Add some Provencal herbs.
4. Place the chicken on the potatoes.
5. Place the grid inside the air fryer.
6. Select 350°F and cook for 40 minutes.
7. Turn the chicken and leave for 15 more minutes.

Nutrition: Calories: 366; Carbohydrates: 40.7 g; Fats: 9.5 g; Protein: 29.7 g

75
Baked Lemon Pepper Chicken Drumsticks

5 minutes | **22 minutes** | **6 drumsticks**

Ingredients

- Olive oil spray
- 6 chicken drumsticks
- 1 tsp lemon pepper
- ½ tsp salt
- ½ tsp granulated garlic
- ½ tsp onion powder

Directions

1. Spray the chicken with olive oil and spray the air fryer basket or line it with parchment paper.
2. In a small bowl, combine the lemon pepper, salt, garlic, and onion powder.
3. Place the chicken in the prepared air fryer basket, and sprinkle with half of the seasoning mixture.
4. Bake at 370°F for 10 minutes.
5. Flip the drumsticks, spray them with more olive oil and sprinkle with the remaining seasoning.
6. Place the chicken back in the air fryer, bake for an additional 12 minutes, and serve.
7. The chicken is done when the internal temperature reaches 180°F and the juices run clear. It should look slightly crisp on the outside.

Nutrition: Calories: 127; Carbohydrates: 0.4 g; Fats: 5.8 g; Protein: 18.3 g

76
Balsamic Glazed Chicken

 5 minutes 22 minutes 4 thighs

Ingredients

GLAZE:
- 1 tbsp olive oil
- 2 tsp balsamic vinegar
- 1 tsp minced garlic
- 1 tsp stevia
- ½ tsp cornstarch
- ¼ tsp salt
- ¼ tsp ground black pepper

CHICKEN:
- Olive oil spray
- 4 bone-in chicken thighs
- 2 tsp granulated garlic
- 1 tsp salt
- ½ tsp ground black pepper
- ¼ tsp onion powder

Directions

MAKE THE GLAZE:
1. In a small bowl, whisk together the olive oil, balsamic vinegar, garlic, stevia, cornstarch, salt, and pepper. Set aside.

MAKE THE CHICKEN:
1. Spray the chicken and the air fryer basket with olive oil.
2. Place the chicken in the air fryer basket, and sprinkle with about half of the garlic, salt, pepper, and onion powder.
3. Bake at 380°F for 10 minutes.
4. Remove the chicken and flip the pieces. Spray with more olive oil, and sprinkle with the remaining seasoning.
5. Place the chicken back in the air fryer and bake for an additional 10 minutes.
6. Remove the chicken and brush with the prepared glaze. Bake for an additional 2 minutes or until the sauce is sticky and caramelized.
7. Serve.

Nutrition: Calories: 178; Carbohydrates: 2.3 g; Fats: 8.3 g; Protein: 23.8 g

77
Chicken Alfredo

 10 minutes   25 – 30 minutes   4

Ingredients

- Some salt
- Freshly ground black pepper
- Freshly chopped parsley, for garnish
- 8 oz fettuccini
- 2 tbsp extra-virgin olive oil
- 2 cloves garlic, minced
- 2 boneless skinless chicken breasts
- ½ cup heavy cream
- 1 cup freshly grated Parmesan
- 1 ½ cup whole milk
- 1 ½ cup low-sodium chicken broth

Directions

1. First, heat the olive oil in the air fryer.
2. Add the chicken and a pinch of salt and pepper.
3. Cook for about 8 minutes until crispy and golden.
4. Take the chicken and let it cool for 10 minutes before you slice it.
5. In the air fryer, mix the garlic with the milk and broth. Add pepper and salt to the mixture.
6. Stir fettuccine into the mixture. Cook it until it becomes thick and firm. This should not take more than 8 minutes. Stir the parmesan and cream into the broth mixture. Leave it for some time to allow it to thicken.
7. Remove the broth from the air fryer and add your slices of chicken. You can now garnish it with parsley.
8. Serve and enjoy!

Nutrition: Calories: 526; Carbohydrates: 49.5 g; Fats: 22.8 g; Protein: 31 g

78
Rolls Stuffed with Broccoli and Carrots with Chicken

15 minutes | 25 minutes | 4

Ingredients

- 8 sheets of rice pasta
- 1 chicken breast
- 1 onion
- 1 carrot
- 150 g broccolis
- 1 can of sweet corn
- Extra virgin olive oil
- Salt
- Ground pepper
- Soy sauce
- 1 bag rice three delicacies

Directions

1. Peel and cut the carrot and cut the broccoli as small as you can. Add the broccoli and carrot to a pot with boiling water and cook for a few minutes. They should be tender but retain a little crunch.
2. Drain well and reserve. Cut the onion into thin slices. Cut the chicken breast into strips.
3. Put some extra virgin olive oil into a wok.
4. When it is hot, add the onion and chicken breast. Sauté well until the chicken is cooked.
5. Drain the corn and add to the wok along with the broccoli and carrot.
6. Sauté so that the ingredients are mixed. Add salt, ground pepper and a little soy sauce.
7. Mix well and let the filling cool. Hydrate the rice pasta sheets.
8. Spread on the worktable and distribute the filling between the sheets of rice paste.
9. Assemble the rolls and paint with a little oil.
10. Put in the air fryer in a single layer. Cook for 10 minutes at 390°F.
11. Then cook at 360°F for 5 minutes.
12. Make the rice as suggested on the packet instruct.
13. Serve the rice with the rolls.

Nutrition: Calories: 223; Fats: 3.5 g; Carbohydrates: 39.5 g; Protein: 11.6 g

79
Spicy Chicken Strips

 5 minutes   12 minutes   5

Ingredients

- 1 cup buttermilk
- 1 ½ tbsp hot pepper sauce
- 1 tsp salt
- ½ tsp black pepper
- 1 pound of boneless and skinless chicken breasts
- ¾ cup panko breadcrumbs
- ½ tsp salt
- ¼ tsp hot pepper, or to taste
- 1 tbsp olive oil

Directions

1. Cut the boneless chicken breast into ¾-inch strips
2. Put the buttermilk, hot sauce, salt and ¼ tsp of black pepper in a shallow bowl.
3. Add the chicken strips and refrigerate for at least two hours. Put breadcrumbs, salt, and the remaining black pepper and hot pepper into another bowl; Add and stir the oil.
4. Remove the chicken strips from the marinade and discard the marinade.
5. Put the strips, a few at the same time, into the crumb mixture. Press the crumbs to the strips to achieve a uniform and firm cover.
6. Put half of the strips in a single layer inside the basket. Cook at 350°F for 12 minutes in the air fryer. Cook the rest when the first batch is cooked.

Nutrition: Calories: 287; Carbohydrates: 9.5 g; Fats: 12.9 g; Protein: 33.4 g

80
Baked Tomato Chicken

 10 minutes   20 minutes   2

Ingredients

- 3 tbsp olive oil
- ½-pint grape tomatoes
- 6 pitted Greek olives, sliced
- 2 boneless skinless chicken breast halves
- ¼ tsp salt
- ¼ tsp pepper
- 2 tbsp capers, drained

Directions

1. Flavor chicken with ground black pepper and salt.
2. Pre-heat the air fryer to 375°F.
3. Take the air fryer basket, and grease it with some cooking spray. Add the chicken to the basket. Add the remaining ingredients and stir.
4. Place the basket in the air fryer
5. Set the temperature to 330°F and set the timer to 15 minutes. Press start.
6. Open the air fryer lid after the cooking time is over. Serve warm.

Nutrition: Calories: 318; Carbohydrates: 5.7 g; Fats: 19.7 g; Protein: 28.7 g

81
Chicken in Tomato Juice

 20 minutes 15 minutes 3

Ingredients

- 350 g chicken fillet
- 200 g tomato juice
- 100 g tomatoes
- 2 tsp basil
- 1 tsp chili
- 1 tsp oregano
- 1 tsp rosemary
- 1 tsp olive oil
- 1 tsp mint
- 1 tsp lemon juice

Directions

1. Take a bowl and make the tomato sauce: combine basil, chili, oregano, rosemary, olive oil, mint and lemon juice and stir the mixture carefully.
2. You can use a hand mixer to help. This will make the mixture smooth.
3. Take a chicken fillet and separate it into 3 pieces.
4. Put the meat into the tomato mixture and leave for 15 minutes.
5. Meanwhile, preheat the air fryer oven to 420°F.
6. Put the meat mixture onto the tray and put it in the oven for at least 15 minutes.

Nutrition: Calories: 154; Protein: 22.7 g; Fats: 4.5 g; Carbohydrates: 5.5 g

82
Chicken Wings with Curry

 15 minutes 20 minutes 4

Ingredients

- 400 g chicken wings
- 30 g curry
- 1 tsp chili
- 1 tsp cayenne pepper
- 1 tsp salt
- 1 lemon
- 1 tsp basil
- 1 tsp oregano
- 3 tsp mustard
- 1 tsp olive oil

Directions

1. Rub the wings with chili, curry, cayenne pepper, salt, basil, and oregano.
2. Add them to the bowl and mix carefully.
3. Leave the mixture for at least 10 minutes in the fridge.
4. Remove the mixture from the fridge. Add mustard and sprinkle with chopped lemon. Stir the mixture gently again.
5. Spray the air fryer pan with olive oil and add the wings.
6. Preheat the air fryer oven to 360°F and add the pan containing the wings.
7. Cook it for 20 minutes.

Nutrition: Calories: 175; Protein: 13.8 g; Fats: 13.6 g; Carbohydrates: 1.2 g

83
Chicken Meatballs

 15 minutes 20 minutes 6

Ingredients

- 400 g ground chicken
- 100 g chopped dill
- 2 tsp olive oil
- 100 g tomato juice
- 1 tsp black pepper
- 1 tsp white pepper
- 1 egg
- 20 g milk

Directions

1. Put the ground chicken into the big mixing bowl.
2. Add the chopped dill and the black and white pepper and stir the mixture carefully.
3. Add the egg and stir again.
4. Make meatballs from the mixture and make the sauce from tomato juice and milk.
5. Pour the sauce into the tray and drop the meatballs in.
6. Preheat the air fryer oven to 360°F and add the meatballs in their tray.
7. Cook for 20 minutes and serve immediately.

Nutrition: Calories: 118; Protein: 15.7 g; Fats: 5.1 g; Carbohydrates: 1.7 g

84
Air Fryer Chicken Wings

 5 minutes 15 minutes 4

Ingredients

- 6 Chicken wings - Flats and drumettes
- Olive oil spray
- Salt
- Pepper
- Barbecue sauce

Directions

1. Spray the air fryer basket or foil-lined air fryer basket with non-stick cooking spray.
2. Arrange the wings equally in the basket.
3. Coat with an even layer of olive oil spray, and add a pinch of salt and pepper to the wings.
4. Pre-heat to 390°F for 10 minutes.
5. Turn and cook for an additional 10 minutes.
6. Using a thermometer, check that the temperature of the wings is at least 165°F.
7. Coat with BBQ sauce if you prefer, or other dipping sauces.

Nutrition: Calories: 136; Protein: 12.7 g; Fats: 9.1 g; Carbohydrates: 1.8 g

85
Spicy Chicken Meatballs

 10 minutes
 11 to 14 minutes
 24

Ingredients

- 1 medium red onion, minced
- 2 garlic cloves, minced
- 1 jalapeño pepper, minced
- 2 tsp olive oil
- 3 tbsp ground almonds
- 1 egg
- 1 tsp dried thyme
- 1 pound of ground chicken breast

Directions

1. In a 6-by-2-inch pan, combine the red onion, garlic, jalapeño, and olive oil. Bake for 3 to 4 minutes in the air fryer, or until the vegetables are crisp but tender. Transfer to a medium bowl.
2. Mix the almonds, egg and thyme into the vegetable mixture. Add the chicken and mix until just combined.
3. Form the chicken mixture into about 24 (1-inch) balls. Bake the meatballs, in batches, for 8 to 10 minutes, until the chicken reaches an internal temperature of 165 °F on a meat thermometer.

Nutrition (one meatball): Calories: 40; Fats: 2.1 g; Protein: 5.2 g; Carbohydrates: 0.3 g

86
Salted Biscuit Pie Turkey Chops

 5 minutes
 20 minutes
 4

Ingredients

- 8 large turkey chops
- 300g crackers
- 2 eggs
- ½ tsp extra virgin olive oil
- Salt to taste
- Ground pepper to taste

Directions

- Put the turkey chops on the worksurface and add salt and pepper.
- Beat the eggs in a bowl.
- Crush the cookies with a blender and then place them in a bowl.
- Coat the chops with the beaten eggs followed by the crushed cookies. Press well so that the empanada is perfect.
- Brush the empanada with olive oil, using a silicone brush.
- Put the chops in the basket of the air fryer, in batches.
- Cook in the air fryer at 400°F for 15 minutes.
- When you have made them all, serve.

Nutrition: Calories: 259; Fats: 7.6 g; Carbohydrates: 12.4 g; Protein: 31.3 g

87
Chicken Wings

 10 minutes   25 minutes   2

Ingredients

- 10 chicken wings (about 700 g)
- Oil spray
- 1 tbsp soy sauce
- ½ tbsp cornstarch
- 2 tbsp maple syrup
- 1 tbsp ground fresh chili paste
- 1 tbsp minced garlic
- ½ tsp chopped fresh ginger
- 1 tbsp lime sumo
- ½ tbsp salt
- 2 tbsp chives

Directions

1. Pat the chicken dry with a tea towel. Cover the chicken with the oil spray.
2. Place the chicken wings inside the air fryer, making sure that they do not overlap each other.
3. Cook at 400°F until the skin is crispy. This should take about 25 minutes. Turn them at the half way point.
4. Mix the soy sauce with cornstarch in a small pan. Add maple syrup, chili paste, garlic, ginger, and lime sumo.
5. Simmer until it boils and thickens.
6. Put chicken in a bowl, add the sauce and cover all the chicken. Sprinkle with chives.

Nutrition: Calories: 451; Fats: 26.4 g; Carbohydrates: 14.5 g; Protein: 37.4 g

88
Mini Turkey Meatballs

15 minutes

10 minutes

5

Ingredients

- 3 tbsp olive oil
- 3 tbsp ketchup
- 3 garlic cloves, minced
- ¼ tsp ground black pepper
- ¼ cup grated Pecorino Romano
- ¼ cup grated Parmesan
- ¼ cup dried breadcrumbs
- ¼ cup Italian parsley leaves, chopped
- 1 tsp salt
- 1 small onion, grated
- 1 pound of ground dark turkey meat
- 1 large egg

Directions

1. Get a big bowl. Add pepper, salt, Pecorino, Parmesan, parsley, ketchup, breadcrumbs, egg, garlic, and onion. Mix them together.
2. Whisk them until they mix evenly. Add the turkey and mix.
3. Shape the mixture into several meatballs. Air fry the meatballs for about 5 minutes until they are brown.
4. Add your meatballs to your favourite sauce.
5. You can now serve the turkey meatballs. They are best served either warm or hot.

Nutrition: Calories: 261; Fats: 13.6 g; Carbohydrates: 9.1 g; Protein: 25.6 g

Chapter 8
SNACK RECIPES

89
Zucchini Crisps

Ingredients

- 2 zucchinis, sliced into a ⅛-inch-thick disks
- A pinch of sea salt
- White pepper to taste
- 1 tbsp olive oil for drizzling

Directions

1. Preheat the air fryer to 330°F.
2. Put the zucchini slices in a bowl with salt. Let them sit in a colander to drain for 30 minutes.
3. Layer the zucchini in a baking dish. Drizzle in oil. Season with pepper. Place the baking dish in the air fryer basket. Cook for 30 minutes.
4. Adjust the seasoning. Serve.

Nutrition: Calories: 35; Carbohydrates: 3.6 g; Fats: 2.1 g; Protein: 0.6 g

90
Skinny Pumpkin Chips

Ingredients

- 1 pound of pumpkin, cut into sticks
- 1 tbsp coconut oil
- ½ tsp rosemary
- ½ tsp basil
- Salt and ground black pepper to taste

Directions

1. Start by preheating the air fryer to 395°F. Brush the pumpkin sticks with coconut oil; add the spices and toss to combine.
2. Cook for 13 minutes, shaking the basket halfway through the cooking time.
3. Serve with mayonnaise. Enjoy!

Nutrition: Calories: 154; Fats: 5.0 g; Carbohydrates: 22.3 g; Protein: 4.2 g

91
Air Fried Ripe Plantains

 10 minutes 10 minutes 2

Ingredients

- 2 pieces of large ripe plantain, peeled and sliced into inch-thick disks
- 1 tbsp coconut unsalted butter or grass-fed butter

Directions

1. Preheat the air fryer to 350°F.
2. Brush a small amount of coconut butter on all sides of the plantain disks.
3. Place one even layer of plantain slices into the air fryer basket, making sure none overlap or touch. Fry the plantains for 10 minutes.
4. Remove from the basket. Place on plates. Repeat these steps for all plantains.
5. While plantains are still warm, serve.

Nutrition: Calories: 200; Carbohydrates: 29 g; Fats: 8 g; Protein: 2.9 g

92
Air Fried Plantains in Coconut Sauce

 10 minutes 10 minutes 4

Ingredients

- 6 ripe plantains, peeled, and quartered lengthwise
- 1 can coconut cream
- 2 tbsp maple syrup
- 1 tbsp coconut oil

Directions

1. Preheat the air fryer to 330°F.
2. Pour coconut cream into a thick-bottomed saucepan set over a high heat; bring to the boil. Reduce the heat to the lowest setting; simmer uncovered until the cream is reduced by half and darkens in color. Turn off the heat.
3. Whisk in maple syrup until smooth. Cool completely before using. Lightly grease a non-stick skillet with coconut oil.
4. Layer plantains in the air fryer basket and fry for 10 minutes or until golden on both sides; drain on paper towels. Place plantain on plates.
5. Drizzle in a small amount of coconut sauce. Serve.

Nutrition: Calories: 284; Carbohydrates: 36.8 g; Fats: 12.5 g; Protein: 4.9 g

93
Cinnamon Pear Chips

15 minutes

9–13 minutes

4

Ingredients

- 2 firm Bosc pears, cut crosswise into ⅛-inch-thick slices
- 1 tbsp freshly squeezed lemon juice
- ½ tsp ground cinnamon
- ⅛ tsp ground cardamom or ground nutmeg

Directions

1. Remove the core and seeds from the larger pear slices. Sprinkle all slices with lemon juice, cinnamon, and cardamom.
2. Put the smaller slices into the basket. Air fry at 380°F for 3 to 5 minutes, until light golden brown, shaking the basket once during cooking. Remove from the air fryer.
3. Repeat with the larger slices, air frying for 6 to 8 minutes, until light golden brown, shaking the basket once during cooking.
4. Remove the slices from the air fryer. Cool and serve or store in an airtight container at room temperature for up to 2 days.

Nutrition: Calories: 35; Fats: 0.1 g; Protein: 0.3 g; Carbohydrates: 8.3 g

94
Air fryer Chicken Nuggets

15 minutes

15 minutes

4

Ingredients

- Olive oil spray
- 2 chicken breasts, skinless, boneless and cut into bite pieces
- ½ tsp salt and freshly ground black pepper to taste
- 2 tbsp grated Parmesan cheese
- 6 tbsp (whole wheat) Italian seasoned breadcrumbs
- 2 tbsp whole wheat breadcrumbs
- 2 tsp olive oil

Directions

1. Pre-heat the air fryer to 400°F
2. Put the cheese and breadcrumbs into a bowl and mix well.
3. Sprinkle salt and pepper on the chicken, add olive oil and mix well.
4. Take a few pieces of chicken and dunk them in the breadcrumb mixture.
5. Put these pieces in an air fryer and spray with olive oil.
6. Cook for 8 minutes, turning halfway through
7. Enjoy with kale chips.

Nutrition: Calories: 188; Carbohydrates: 8.1 g; Protein: 24.5 g; Fats: 4.5 g

95
Air fryer Sweet Potato Fries

 5 minutes   8 minutes   2

Ingredients

- 1 sweet potato
- Pinch salt and ground black pepper
- 1 tsp olive oil

Directions

1. Cut the peeled sweet potato into French fries. Coat with salt, pepper, and oil.
2. Cook in the air fryer. Cook potatoes in batches, in single layers.
3. Shake once or twice.
4. Serve with your favorite sauce.

Nutrition: Calories: 106; Carbohydrates: 13.2 g; Protein: 1.1 g; Fats: 5.6 g

96
Air fryer Kale Chips

 5 minutes   5 minutes   2

Ingredients

- 1 bunch kale
- ½ tsp garlic powder
- 1 tsp olive oil
- ½ tsp salt

Directions

1. Preheat the air fryer to 370°F.
2. Cut the kale into small pieces without the stem.
3. Put all the ingredients in a bowl with the kale pieces.
4. Take out the kale and add to the air fryer.
5. Cook for three minutes. Toss and cook for two minutes more.
6. Serve with any dipping.

Nutrition: Calories: 52; Carbohydrates: 6 g; Protein: 1.3 g; Fats: 2.5 g

97
Spiced Apples

 5 minutes 17 minutes 4

Ingredients

- 4 small apples, cored, sliced
- 2 tbsp Erythritol sweetener
- 1 tsp apple pie spice
- 2 tbsp olive oil

Directions

1. Switch on the air fryer. Insert the fryer basket and spray with olive oil. Pre-heat the air fryer to 350°F.
2. Meanwhile, place the apple slices in a bowl, sprinkle with sweetener and spice, drizzle with oil and stir until evenly coated.
3. Open the fryer, add apple slices and cook for 12 minutes until nicely golden and crispy. Shake halfway through the frying.
4. Serve straight away.

Nutrition: Calories: 120; Carbohydrates: 15.8 g; Fats: 6.2 g; Protein: 0.5 g

98
Cinnamon Toasted Almonds

 5 minutes 25 minutes 8

Ingredients

- 2 cups whole almonds
- 1 tbsp olive oil
- 1 tsp ground cinnamon
- ½ tsp salt

Directions

1. Preheat the air fryer to 325°F and insert the fryer basket.
2. Toss together the almonds, olive oil, cinnamon, and salt.
3. Spread the almonds on the basket.
4. Bake for 25 minutes, stirring several times until toasted.

Nutrition: Calories: 81; Carbohydrates: 3.3 g; Fats: 8.6 g; Protein: 2.5 g

99
Avocado Fries with Roasted Garlic Mayonnaise

 50 minutes   1 hour   4

Ingredients

- ¾ cup of all-purpose flour
- Salt and black pepper to taste
- 2 eggs
- 1 cup tortilla chips, crushed
- 3 avocados, cut into wedges

SAUCE:
- ½ cup mayonnaise
- 1 tsp lemon juice
- 1 tsp mustard
- ½ head of garlic (you will need about 6-7 cloves)

Directions

1. Preheat the air fryer at 400°F.
2. Put the garlic on a piece of aluminum foil and drizzle with cooking spray. Wrap it in the foil.
3. Cook the garlic in the air fryer for 12 minutes. Check the garlic, open the top of the foil, and continue to cook for 10 minutes more.
4. Let it rest for 10 to 15 minutes; remove the cloves by squeezing them out of the skins; mash the garlic and put to one side.
5. In a shallow bowl, combine the flour, salt, and black pepper. In another shallow dish, whisk the eggs until frothy.
6. Place the crushed tortilla chips in a third shallow dish. Dip the avocado wedges in the flour mixture, shaking off the excess. Then, dip in the egg mixture, followed by the crushed tortilla chips.
7. Sprinkle the avocado wedges with cooking oil on all sides.
8. Cook in the preheated air fryer at 395°F for approximately 8 minutes, turning them over halfway through the cooking time.
9. Meanwhile, combine the sauce ingredients with the smashed roasted garlic. To serve, divide the avocado fries between plates and top with the sauce. Enjoy!

Nutrition: Calories: 351; Fats: 26.7 g; Carbohydrates: 21.5 g; Protein: 6.4 g

100
Chili Fingerling Potatoes

 10 minutes   16 minutes   4

Ingredients

- 1 pound fingerling potatoes, rinsed and cut into wedges
- 1 tsp olive oil
- 1 tsp salt
- 1 tsp black pepper
- 1 tsp cayenne pepper
- 1 tsp nutritional yeast
- ½ tsp garlic powder

Directions

1. Preheat the air fryer to 400°F.
2. Coat the potatoes with the rest of the ingredients and put them in the air fryer basket.
3. Cook them for 16 minutes, shaking the basket halfway through the cooking time.
4. Serve immediately.

Nutrition: Calories: 116; Carbohydrates: 23.2 g; Fats: 2.4 g; Protein: 2.1 g

Chapter 9
VEGETABLE AND VEGETARIAN RECIPES

101
Delicata Squash

Ingredients

- ½ tbsp olive oil
- 1 delicata squash
- ½ tsp salt
- ½ tsp Rosemary

Directions

1. Chop the squash into slices of ¼ thickness. Discard the seeds.
2. Put olive oil, salt, rosemary and the squash slices in a bowl. Mix well.
3. Cook the squash for 10 minutes at 400°F in the air fryer. Flip the squash halfway through.
4. Make sure they are cooked completely.
5. Serve hot.

Nutrition: Calories: 86; Carbohydrates: 13.7 g; Fats: 5.1 g; Protein: 1.9 g

102
Spicy Glazed Carrots

Ingredients

- 1-pound carrots, cut into matchsticks
- 2 tbsp peanut oil
- 1 tbsp agave syrup
- 1 jalapeño, seeded and minced
- ¼ tsp dill
- ½ tsp basil
- Salt and white pepper to taste

Directions

1. Preheat your air fryer to 380°F.
2. Toss all the ingredients together and place them in the air fryer basket.
3. Prepare for 15 minutes, shaking the basket halfway through the cooking time. Transfer to a serving platter and enjoy!

Nutrition: Calories: 162; Fats: 9.3 g; Carbohydrates: 20.1 g; Protein: 1.4 g

103
Corn on the Cob with Herb 'Butter'

15 minutes | 10 minutes | 2

Ingredients

- 2 ears of new corn, shucked and cut into halves
- 2 tbsp oil
- 1 tsp granulated garlic
- ½ tsp fresh ginger, grated
- Sea salt and pepper, to taste
- 1 tbsp fresh rosemary, chopped
- 1 tbsp fresh basil, chopped
- 2 tbsp fresh chives, roughly chopped

Directions

1. Spritz the corn with cooking spray. Cook at 395°F for 6 minutes, turning them over halfway through the cooking time.
2. Meanwhile, mix the butter with the granulated garlic, ginger, salt, black pepper, rosemary, and basil.
3. Spread the butter mixture all over the corn on the cob. Cook in the preheated air fryer for an additional 2 minutes. Bon appétit!

Nutrition: Calories: 225; Fats: 9.3 g; Carbohydrates: 30.2 g; Protein: 5.4 g

104
Sesame Seeds Bok Choy

10 minutes | 6 minutes | 4

Ingredients

- 4 bunches of baby bok choy, bottoms removed and leaves separated
- Olive oil cooking spray
- 1 tsp garlic powder
- 1 tsp sesame seeds

Directions

1. Set the temperature of the air fryer to 325°F.
2. Arrange bok choy leaves in the air fryer basket in a single layer.
3. Spray with the cooking spray and sprinkle with garlic powder.
4. Air fry for about 5-6 minutes, shaking after every 2 minutes.
5. Remove from the air fryer and transfer the bok choy onto serving plates.
6. Garnish with sesame seeds and serve hot.

Nutrition: Calories: 36; Carbohydrates: 6.0 g; Protein: 1.5 g; Fats: 0.7 g

105
Sweet-and-Sour Mixed Veggies

 25 minutes 10 minutes 4

Ingredients

- ½-pound sterling asparagus, cut into 1 ½-inch pieces
- ½-pound broccoli, cut into 1 ½-inch pieces
- ½-pound carrots, cut into 1 ½-inch pieces
- 2 tbsp of peanut oil
- Some salt and white pepper, to taste
- ½ cup water
- 4 tbsp raisins
- 2 tbsp maple syrup
- 2 tbsp apple cider vinegar

Directions

1. Put the vegetables in a single layer in the lightly greased cooking basket. Drizzle the peanut oil over the vegetables.
2. Sprinkle with salt and white pepper.
3. Cook at 380°F for 15 minutes, shaking the basket halfway through the cooking time.
4. Add ½ cup of water to a saucepan; bring it to a rapid boil, and add the raisins, maple syrup, and vinegar. Prepare for 5 to 7 minutes or until the sauce has been reduced by half.
5. Spoon the sauce over the warm vegetables and serve immediately. Bon appétit!

Nutrition: Calories: 163; Fats: 7.1 g; Carbohydrates: 21.6 g; Protein: 3.6 g

106
Roast Eggplant and Zucchini Bites

 35 minutes 30 minutes 8

Ingredients

- 2 tsp fresh mint leaves, chopped
- 1 ½ tsp red pepper chili flakes
- 1 pound (454 g) eggplant, peeled and cubed
- 1 pound (454 g) zucchini, peeled and cubed
- 3 tbsp olive oil

Directions

1. Toss all of the above ingredients in a large-sized mixing dish.
2. Roast the eggplant and zucchini bites for 30 minutes at 325°F in your air fryer, turning once or twice.
3. Serve with a homemade dipping sauce.

Nutrition: Calories: 68; Fats: 2.5 g; Protein: 2.6 g; Carbohydrates: 8.8 g

107
Basil Tomatoes

Ingredients

- 2 tomatoes, halved
- Olive oil cooking spray
- Salt and ground black pepper, as required
- 1 tbsp fresh basil, chopped

Directions

1. Set the temperature of the air fryer to 320°F. Grease an air fryer basket.
2. Spray the tomato halves evenly with cooking spray and sprinkle with salt, black pepper and basil.
3. Arrange tomato halves in the prepared air fryer basket, cut sides up.
4. Air fry for about 10 minutes or until they are done to your taste.
5. Remove from the air fryer and transfer the tomatoes onto serving plates.
6. Serve warm.

Nutrition: Calories: 42; Carbohydrates: 4.8 g; Protein: 1.1 g; Fats: 1.8 g

108
Stuffed Tomatoes

Ingredients

- 4 tomatoes & 1 tsp olive oil
- 1 carrot, peeled and finely chopped
- 1 onion, chopped
- 1 cup frozen peas, thawed
- 1 garlic clove, minced
- 2 cups cold-cooked rice
- 1 tbsp soy sauce

Directions

1. Cut the top of each tomato and scoop out pulp and seeds.
2. In a skillet, heat oil over low heat and sauté the carrot, onion, garlic, and peas for about 2 minutes. Stir in the soy sauce and rice and remove from heat.
3. Set the temperature of the air fryer to 355°F. Grease an air fryer basket.
4. Stuff each tomato with the rice mixture.
5. Arrange tomatoes in the prepared air fryer basket.
6. Air fry for about 20 minutes.
7. Remove from the air fryer and transfer the tomatoes onto a serving platter.
8. Set aside to cool slightly. Serve warm.

Nutrition: Calories: 241; Carbohydrates: 50.1 g; Protein: 7.5 g; Fats: 1.2 g

109
Spicy Potatoes

Ingredients

- 1 ¾ pound of waxy potatoes, peeled and cubed
- ½ tbsp olive oil
- ½ tsp ground cumin
- ½ tsp ground coriander
- ½ tsp paprika
- Salt and freshly ground black pepper, as required

Directions

1. Put the cubed potatoes in a large bowl of water and set them to one side for about 30 minutes.
2. Drain the potatoes completely and dry with paper towels.
3. Put the potatoes, oil, and spices in another bowl and toss to coat well.
4. Set the temperature of the air fryer to 355°F. Grease an air fryer basket.
5. Arrange the potato pieces in the prepared air fryer basket in a single layer.
6. Air fry for about 20 minutes.
7. Remove from the air fryer and transfer the potato pieces onto serving plates.
8. Serve hot.

Nutrition: Calories: 113; Carbohydrates: 21 g; Protein: 2.3 g; Fats: 2.5 g

110
Roasted Okra

Ingredients

- ½ lb. okra, ends trimmed and pods sliced
- ¼ tsp salt
- ¼ tsp olive oil
- ⅛ tsp ground black pepper

Directions

1. Preheat your air fryer to 350°F.
2. Mix the okra, salt, olive oil, and pepper in a bowl. Stir the mixture gently.
3. Place them in a single layer in the air fryer basket.
4. Allow them to cook in the air fryer for 5 minutes.
5. Toss and cook for an additional 5 minutes.
6. Toss again and allow them to cook for an extra 2 minutes.
7. Withdraw and serve instantly.

Nutrition: Calories: 73; Protein: 4.8 g; Fats: 1.0 g; Carbohydrates: 11.2 g

111
Hasselback Potatoes

15 minutes | 30 minutes | 4

Ingredients

- 4 potatoes
- 2 tbsp olive oil
- 1 tbsp fresh chives, chopped

Directions

1. With a sharp knife, cut slits across each potato, about ¼-inch apart, making sure that the slices stay connected at the bottom.
2. Preheat the temperature of the air fryer to 355°F.
3. After preheating, arrange the potatoes in the greased air fryer basket.
4. Slide the basket into the air fryer and set the time for 30 minutes.
5. Halfway through cooking, coat the potatoes with oil.
6. When the cooking time is completed, open the lid and transfer the potatoes onto a platter.
7. Garnish with the chives and serve immediately.

Nutrition: Calories: 195; Fats: 5.2 g; Carbohydrates: 33.5 g; Protein: 3.6 g

112
Glazed Carrots

10 minutes | 12 minutes | 4

Ingredients

- 3 cups carrots, peeled and cut into large chunks
- 1 tbsp olive oil
- 1 tbsp maple syrup
- 1 tbsp fresh thyme, finely chopped
- Salt and ground black pepper, as required

Directions

1. Put the carrot, oil, maple syrup, thyme, salt and black pepper in a bowl and mix until well combined.
2. Set the temperature of the air fryer to 390°F and preheat for 5 minutes.
3. After preheating, arrange the carrot chunks in the greased air fryer basket in a single layer.
4. Slide the basket into the air fryer and set the timer for 12 minutes.
5. When the cooking time is completed, open the lid and transfer the carrot chunks onto serving plates.
6. Serve hot.

Nutrition: Calories: 79; Fats: 3.6 g; Carbohydrates: 11.9 g; Protein: 0.7 g

113
Spicy Green Beans

10 minutes | 24 minutes | 3

Ingredients

- 1 garlic clove, minced
- 1 tsp soy sauce
- 1 tbsp sesame oil
- 1 tsp rice wine vinegar
- ½ tsp red pepper flakes
- 12 oz fresh green beans, trimmed

Directions

1. Put all of the ingredients in a bowl, except for the green beans, and beat until they are well combined.
2. Add the green beans and toss to coat well.
3. Set aside for about 5 minutes.
4. Preheat the air fryer to 400°F
5. After preheating, arrange the green beans in the greased air fryer basket in 2 batches.
6. Slide the basket into the air fryer and set the timer for 12 minutes.
7. When cooking time is completed, transfer the green beans onto a platter.
8. Serve hot.

Nutrition: Calories: 77; Fats: 3.7 g; Carbohydrates: 8.7 g; Protein: 2.3 g

114
Soy Sauce Mushrooms

10 minutes | 10 minutes | 2

Ingredients

- 1 (8-oz) package Cremini mushrooms, sliced
- 2 tbsp avocado oil
- 1 tsp low-sodium soy sauce
- ½ tsp garlic granules
- Salt and ground black pepper, as required

Directions

1. In a bowl, add all ingredients and toss to coat well.
2. Set the temperature of the air fryer to 375°F to preheat for 5 minutes.
3. After preheating, arrange the mushrooms into the greased air fryer Basket.
4. Slide the basket into the air fryer and set the time for 10 minutes.
5. While cooking, shake the air fryer basket occasionally.
6. Serve hot.

Nutrition: Calories: 142; Fats: 10.1 g; Carbohydrates: 8.9 g; Protein: 3.9 g

115
Braised Mushrooms

Ingredients

- 1 tbsp coconut oil
- 2 tsp Herbs de Provence
- ½ tsp garlic powder
- 2 pounds fresh mushrooms, quartered

Directions

1. Put all the ingredients in a bowl and mix well.
2. Set the temperature of the air fryer to 320°F to preheat for 5 minutes.
3. After preheating, add all the ingredients to the air fryer pan.
4. Slide the pan into the air fryer and cook for 30 minutes.
5. Serve hot.

Nutrition: Calories: 77; Fats: 2.7 g; Carbohydrates: 8.3 g; Protein: 4.8 g

116
Lemony Spinach

Ingredients

- 2 pounds of fresh spinach, chopped
- 1 garlic clove, minced
- 1 jalapeño pepper, minced
- 2 tbsp olive oil
- Salt and ground black pepper, as required
- 1 tbsp fresh lemon juice
- 1 tsp fresh lemon zest, grated

Directions

1. Put the spinach, garlic, jalapeño, oil, salt and black pepper in a bowl and mix well.
2. Set the temperature of the air fryer to 340°F and preheat for 5 minutes.
3. After preheating, arrange the spinach mixture in the greased air fryer basket.
4. Slide the basket into the air fryer and set the time for 15 minutes.
5. When the cooking time is completed, transfer the spinach mixture into a bowl.
6. Immediately stir in the lemon juice and zest and serve hot.

Nutrition: Calories: 89; Fats: 5.3 g; Carbohydrates: 5.9 g; Protein: 4.4 g

117
Buffalo Cauliflower Wings

 5 minutes 30 minutes 6

Ingredients

- 1 tbsp almond flour
- 1 medium head cauliflower
- 1 ½ tsp salt
- 4 tbsp hot sauce
- 1 tbsp olive oil

Directions

1. Switch on the air fryer and insert the fryer basket. Grease it with olive oil, set the fryer to 400°F and preheat for 5 minutes.
2. Meanwhile, cut the cauliflower into bite-size florets and set it to one side.
3. Place the flour in a large bowl and then whisk in the salt, oil, and hot sauce until they are combined. Add the cauliflower florets and toss until combined.
4. Open the fryer and add the cauliflower florets in a single layer. Cook them for 15 minutes until nicely golden and crispy, shaking halfway through the frying.
5. When the air fryer beeps, transfer the cauliflower florets onto a serving plate and keep warm.
6. Cook the remaining cauliflower florets the same way and serve.

Nutrition: Calories: 83; Carbohydrates: 12.2 g; Fats: 3.4 g; Protein: 1.0 g

118
Sweet Potato Cauliflower Patties

20 minutes | 40 minutes | 7

Ingredients

- 1 green onion, chopped
- 1 large sweet potato, peeled
- 1 tsp minced garlic
- 1 cup cilantro leaves
- 2 cups cauliflower florets
- ¼ tsp ground black pepper
- ¼ tsp salt
- ¼ cup sunflower seeds
- ¼ tsp cumin
- ¼ cup ground flaxseed
- ½ tsp red chili powder
- 2 tbsp ranch seasoning mix
- 2 tbsp arrowroot starch

Directions

1. Cut the peeled sweet potato into small pieces, then place them in a food processor and pulse until the pieces are broken up.
2. Then add onion, cauliflower florets, and garlic. Pulse until they are combined. Add the remaining ingredients and then pulse more until they are well combined.
3. Tip the mixture into a bowl, shape the mixture into seven 1 ½ inch thick patties, each about ¼ cup, then place them on a baking sheet and freeze for 10 minutes.
4. Switch on the air fryer. Insert the fryer basket, grease it with olive and then preheat it at 400°F for 10 minutes.
5. Open the fryer, add patties to it in a single layer and then cook for 20 minutes until nicely golden and cooked. Flip the patties halfway through frying.
6. When the air fryer beeps, transfer the patties onto a serving plate, and keep them warm.
7. Prepare the remaining patties in the same way and serve.

Nutrition: Calories: 81; Carbohydrates: 9.2 g; Fats: 3.7 g; Protein: 2.7 g

119
Fried Peppers with Sriracha Mayo

 20 minutes 10 minutes 2

Ingredients

- 4 bell peppers, seeded and sliced (1-inch pieces)
- 1 onion, sliced (1-inch pieces)
- 1 tbsp olive oil
- ½ tsp dried rosemary
- ½ tsp dried basil
- salt, to taste
- ¼ tsp ground black pepper
- ⅓ cup vegan mayonnaise
- ⅓ tsp Sriracha

Directions

1. Toss the bell peppers and onions with olive oil, rosemary, basil, salt, and black pepper.
2. Place the peppers and onions in the cooking basket in an even layer. Cook at 400°F for 12 to 14 minutes.
3. Meanwhile, make the sauce by whisking the vegan mayonnaise and Sriracha. Serve immediately.

Nutrition: Calories: 264; Fats: 24.1 g; Carbohydrates: 9.5 g; Protein: 2.3 g

120
Spicy Roasted Potatoes

 15 minutes 10 minutes 2

Ingredients

- 4 potatoes, peeled and cut into wedges
- 2 tbsp olive oil
- Salt and black pepper to taste
- 1 tsp cayenne pepper
- ½ tsp ancho chili powder

Directions

1. Toss all the ingredients in a mixing bowl until the potatoes are well covered.
2. Transfer them to the air fryer basket and cook at 400°F for 6 minutes; shake the basket and cook for a further 6 minutes.
3. Serve with your favorite sauce for dipping. Bon appétit!

Nutrition: Calories: 354; Fats: 7.6 g; Carbohydrates: 59.9 g; Protein: 6.8 g

121
Okra

Ingredients

- 1 cup almond flour
- 8 oz fresh okra
- ½ tsp sea salt
- 1 cup milk, reduced-fat
- 1 egg, pastured

Directions

1. Break the egg into a bowl, pour in the milk and then whisk until blended.
2. Cut the stem from each okra, then cut it into ½-inch pieces. Next, add these to the eggs and stir until well coated.
3. Mix flour and salt and put in a large plastic bag.
4. Working on one okra piece at a time, drain the okra well by letting excess egg drip off. Next, add each piece to the flour mixture then seal the bag and shake well until each okra piece is well coated.
5. Place the coated okra on a greased air fryer basket. Coat the remaining okra pieces the same way and place them in the basket.
6. Switch on the air fryer and insert the fryer basket. Spray the okra with oil, then cook at 390°F for 10 minutes until nicely golden and cooked. Stir the okra halfway through the frying.
7. Serve straight away.

Nutrition: Calories: 134; Carbohydrates: 15.8 g; Fats: 4.9 g; Protein: 7.3 g

122
Cauliflower Rice

10 minutes | 27 minutes | 3

Ingredients

FOR THE TOFU:
- 1 cup diced carrot
- 6 oz tofu, extra-firm, drained
- ½ cup diced white onion
- 2 tbsp soy sauce
- 1 tsp turmeric

FOR THE CAULIFLOWER:
- ½ cup chopped broccoli
- 3 cup cauliflower rice
- 1 tbsp minced garlic
- ½ cup frozen peas
- 1 tbsp minced ginger
- 2 tbsp soy sauce
- 1 tbsp apple cider vinegar
- 1 ½ tsp toasted sesame oil

Directions

1. Switch on the air fryer. Insert the fryer basket, grease it with olive and then preheat it at 370°F for 5 minutes.
2. Meanwhile, place the tofu in a bowl, crumble it and then add the remaining ingredients. Stir until everything is well mixed.
3. Open the fryer, add the tofu mixture to it and spray with oil. Cook for 10 minutes until nicely golden and crispy, stirring halfway through the frying.
4. Meanwhile, place all the ingredients for the cauliflower in a bowl and toss until mixed.
5. When the air fryer beeps, add the cauliflower mixture, shaking the pan gently to mix. Continue cooking for 12 minutes, shaking halfway through the frying.
6. Serve straight away.

Nutrition: Calories: 279; Carbohydrates: 27.8 g; Fats: 13 g; Protein: 14.2 g

123
Asparagus Avocado Soup

 10 minutes   20 minutes   4

Ingredients

- 1 avocado, peeled, pitted, cubed
- 12 oz asparagus
- ½ tsp ground black pepper
- 1 tsp garlic powder
- 1 tsp sea salt
- 2 tbsp olive oil
- ½ lemon, juiced
- 2 cups vegetable stock

Directions

1. Switch on the air fryer and insert the fryer basket. Grease it with olive oil and then preheat it to 425°F for 5 minutes.
2. Meanwhile, place the asparagus in a shallow dish and drizzle with 1 tbsp oil. Sprinkle with garlic powder, salt, and black pepper and toss until well mixed.
3. Add asparagus to the fryer and cook for 10 minutes until nicely golden and roasted, shaking halfway through the frying.
4. When the air fryer beeps, transfer the asparagus to a food processor.
5. Add the remaining ingredients to a food processor and pulse until well combined and smooth.
6. Tip the soup into a saucepan and pour in water. If the soup is too thick, heat it over medium-low heat for 5 minutes until thoroughly heated.
7. Ladle soup into bowls and serve.

Nutrition: Calories: 195; Carbohydrates: 15.3 g; Fats: 8.6 g; Protein: 6.4 g

124
Roasted Broccoli with Sesame Seeds

 15 minutes   10 minutes   2

Ingredients

- 1 pound broccoli florets
- 2 tbsp sesame oil
- ½ tsp shallot powder
- ½ tsp porcini powder
- 1 tsp garlic powder
- Salt and pepper to taste
- ½ tsp cumin powder
- ¼ tsp paprika
- 2 tbsp sesame seeds

Directions

1. Start by warming the Air fryer to 400°F.
2. Blanch the broccoli in salted boiling water until al dente, about 3 to 4 minutes. Drain well and transfer to the lightly greased air fryer basket.
3. Add the sesame oil, shallot powder, porcini powder, garlic powder, salt, black pepper, cumin powder, paprika, and sesame seeds.
4. Cook for 6 minutes, tossing them over halfway through the cooking time. Bon appétit!

Nutrition: Calories: 229; Fats: 14.5 g; Carbohydrates: 18.2 g; Protein: 6.9 g

125
Crispy Tofu

30 minutes   15 to 20 minutes   4

Ingredients

- 1 (16-oz / 454-g) block extra-firm tofu
- 2 tbsp coconut aminos
- 1 tbsp toasted sesame oil
- 1 tbsp olive oil
- 1 tbsp chili-garlic sauce
- 1 ½ tsp black sesame seeds
- 1 scallion, thinly sliced

Directions

1. Press the tofu for at least 15 minutes by wrapping it in paper towels and setting a heavy pan on top so that the moisture drains.
2. Slice the tofu into bite-size cubes and transfer them to a bowl. Drizzle with coconut aminos, sesame oil, olive oil, and chili-garlic sauce. Cover and refrigerate for 1 hour or up to overnight. Preheat the air fryer to 400°F.
3. Arrange the tofu in a single layer in the air fryer basket. Shake the pan halfway through the cooking time. Air fry for 15 to 20 minutes until crisp. Serve with any juices that accumulate in the bottom of the air fryer, sprinkled with the sesame seeds and sliced scallion.

Nutrition: Calories: 173; Fats: 10.3 g; Protein: 16.8 g; Carbohydrates: 4.5 g

126
Kale with Pine Nuts

15 minutes | 15 minutes | 3

Ingredients

- 1 pound fresh kale, tough ribs removed and chopped
- 2 tbsp olive oil
- ¼ tsp ground cumin
- ¼ tsp red pepper flakes, crushed
- Salt and ground black pepper, as required
- 2 tbsp pine nuts
- ½ tbsp fresh lime juice

Directions

1. In a bowl, add the kale, oil, spices, salt and black pepper and mix well.
2. Set the temperature of the air fryer to 340°F to preheat for 5 minutes.
3. After preheating, arrange the kale in the greased air fryer basket.
4. Slide the basket into the air fryer and set the time for 15 minutes.
5. When the cooking time is completed, open the lid and immediately transfer the kale mixture into a bowl.
6. Stir in the pine nuts and lime juice and serve hot.

Nutrition: Calories: 176; Fats: 10.4 g; Carbohydrates: 17 g; Protein: 3.5 g

127
Spiced Sweet Potatoes

10 minutes | 20 minutes | 4

Ingredients

- 3 large sweet potatoes, peeled and cut into 1-inch cubes
- 2 tbsp vegetable oil
- ¼ tsp dried parsley
- ½ tsp ground cumin
- ½ tsp red chili powder
- Salt and ground black pepper, as required

Directions

1. Put all the ingredients in a large bowl and toss to coat well.
2. Set the temperature of the air fryer to 415°F to preheat for 5 minutes.
3. After preheating, arrange the sweet potato cubes in the greased air fryer basket in a single layer.
4. Slide the basket into the air fryer and set the time for 20 minutes.
5. When the cooking time is completed, transfer the sweet potato cubes to a bowl.
6. Serve hot.

Nutrition: Calories: 198; Fats: 6.1 g; Carbohydrates: 33.4 g; Protein: 1.9 g

128
Glazed Broccoli

Ingredients

- 1 pound broccoli, cut into florets
- 1 tbsp garlic, minced
- 1 ½ tbsp peanut oil
- Salt, as required
- 2 tbsp low-sodium soy sauce
- 2 tsp Sriracha
- 2 tsp maple syrup
- 1 tsp rice vinegar
- ⅓ cup salted peanuts, roasted

Directions

1. Put the broccoli florets, garlic, peanut oil and salt in a large bowl and toss to coat well.
2. Set the temperature of the air fryer to 400°F to preheat for 5 minutes.
3. After preheating, arrange the broccoli florets in the greased air fryer basket in a single layer.
4. Cook for 20 minutes, tossing the broccoli florets halfway through.
5. Meanwhile, put the maple syrup, soy sauce, sriracha and vinegar in a small, microwave-safe bowl and mix well.
6. Microwave on high for about 10-15 seconds until the maple syrup is melted.
7. Remove from the microwave and stir until smooth.
8. When the cooking time is completed, remove the broccoli florets and transfer them into a large bowl.
9. Add the maple syrup mixture and toss to coat well.
10. Add the peanuts and stir to combine.
11. Serve immediately.

Nutrition: Calories: 219; Fats: 13.9 g; Carbohydrates: 17.4 g; Protein: 6.7 g

129
Green Beans with Carrots

 15 minutes   10 minutes   4

Ingredients

- ½ pound green beans, trimmed
- ½ pound carrots, peeled and cut into
- 1 tbsp olive oil
- Salt and ground black pepper, as required

Directions

1. Put all the ingredients in a bowl and toss to coat well.
2. Set the temperature of the air fryer to 400°F to preheat for 5 minutes.
3. After preheating, arrange the carrot mixture in the greased air fryer basket.
4. Slide the basket into the air fryer and cook for 10 minutes.
5. Serve hot.

Nutrition: Calories: 84; Fats: 2.8 g; Carbohydrates: 13.8 g; Protein: 2.0 g

130
Broccoli with Cauliflower

 15 minutes   20 minutes   2

Ingredients

- 1 ½ cup broccoli, cut into 1-inch pieces
- 1 ½ cup cauliflower, cut into 1-inch pieces
- 1 tbsp olive oil
- Salt, as required

Directions

1. Put the vegetables, oil, and salt in a bowl and toss to coat well.
2. Set the temperature of the air fryer to 375°F to preheat for 5 minutes.
3. After preheating, arrange the veggie mixture into the greased air fryer basket.
4. Slide the basket into the air fryer and set the time for 20 minutes.
5. Toss the veggie mixture once halfway through.
6. When the cooking time is completed, transfer the veggie mixture into a bowl.
7. Serve hot.

Nutrition: Calories: 92; Fats: 5.3 g; Carbohydrates: 8.5 g; Protein: 3.4 g

131
Mushroom with Green Peas

Ingredients

- ½ cup low-sodium soy sauce
- 4 tbsp rice vinegar
- 4 tbsp maple syrup
- 4 garlic cloves, finely chopped
- 2 tsp Chinese five-spice powder
- ½ tsp ground ginger
- 16 oz fresh mushrooms, halved
- ½ cup frozen green peas

Directions:

1. Put the soy sauce, maple syrup, vinegar, garlic, five-spice powder, and ground ginger in a bowl and mix well.
2. Set the temperature of the air fryer to 350°F to preheat for 5 minutes.
3. After preheating, arrange the mushrooms in the greased air fryer pan.
4. Slide the pan into the air fryer and set the time for 15 minutes.
5. After 10 minutes of cooking in the pan, add the green peas and vinegar mixture and stir to combine. When the cooking time is completed, transfer the mushroom mixture into a bowl. Serve hot.

Nutrition: Calories: 124; Fats: 0.4 g; Carbohydrates: 23.2 g; Protein: 6.8 g

132
Carrot with Zucchini

Ingredients

- 6 tsp olive oil
- ½ pound carrots, peeled and sliced
- 2 pounds zucchinis, sliced
- 1 tbsp fresh basil, chopped
- Salt and ground black pepper, as required

Directions

1. In a bowl, mix together 2 tsp of oil and carrots.
2. Set the temperature of the air fryer to 400°F for 5 minutes.
3. After preheating, place the carrots in the greased air fryer basket in a single layer.
4. Slide the basket into air fryer and set the time for 35 minutes.
5. Meanwhile, in a large bowl, mix together the remaining oil, zucchini, basil, salt and black pepper.
6. After 5 minutes of cooking, place the zucchini mixture into the basket with the carrots.
7. While cooking, toss the vegetable mixture 2-3 times.
8. When the cooking time is completed, transfer the carrot mixture into a bowl.
9. Serve hot.

Nutrition: Calories: 187; Fats: 10.2 g; Carbohydrates: 20.8 g; Protein: 2.2 g

133
Potato with Bell Peppers

 14 minutes   25 minutes   2

Ingredients

- 2 cups water
- 5 russet potatoes, peeled and cubed
- ½ tbsp extra-virgin olive oil
- ½ onion, chopped
- ½ jalapeño pepper, chopped
- ½ red bell pepper, seeded and chopped
- ½ green bell pepper, seeded and chopped
- ¼ tbsp dried oregano, crushed
- ¼ tbsp garlic powder
- ¼ tbsp ground cumin
- ¼ tbsp red chili powder
- Salt and ground black pepper, as required

Directions

1. Put the water and potatoes in a large bowl and set aside for about 30 minutes.
2. Drain well and pat dry with paper towels.
3. Add the potatoes and oil to a bowl and toss to coat well.
4. Set the temperature of the air fryer to 330°F to preheat for 5 minutes.
5. After preheating, place the potatoes into an air fryer basket.
6. Slide the basket into the air fryer and set the time for 5 minutes
7. Transfer the potatoes onto a wire rack to cool.
8. In the same bowl, add all the remaining ingredients and toss to coat well.
9. Now, set the temperature of the air fryer to 390°F to preheat for 5 minutes.
10. Add the cooled potatoes to the veggie mixture and toss to coat well
11. Place the potato mixture in the air fryer basket.
12. Slide the basket into the air fryer and cook for 15-20 minutes or until it is done to your taste.
13. When the cooking time is completed, transfer the veggie mixture into a bowl.
14. Serve hot.

Nutrition: Calories: 211; Fats: 2.3 g; Carbohydrates: 46.4 g; Protein: 3.2 g

134
Veggie Ratatouille

 15 minutes 15 minutes 2

Ingredients

- 1 green bell pepper, seeded and chopped
- 1 yellow bell pepper, seeded and chopped
- 1 eggplant, chopped
- 1 zucchini, chopped
- 3 tomatoes, chopped
- 2 small onions, chopped
- 2 garlic cloves, minced
- 2 tbsp Herbs de Provence
- 1 tbsp olive oil
- 1 tbsp balsamic vinegar
- Salt and ground black pepper, as required

Directions

1. Put the vegetables, garlic, herbs de Provence, oil, vinegar, salt, and black pepper in a bowl and toss to coat well.
2. Set the temperature of the air fryer to 355°F to preheat for 5 minutes.
3. After preheating, place the vegetable mixture in the air fryer pan and place inside the air fryer.
4. After 25 minutes of cooking, add the wine to the pan and stir with the mushroom mixture.
5. Serve hot.

Nutrition: Calories: 142; Fats: 5.2 g; Carbohydrates: 20.3 g; Protein: 3.6 g

135
Seasoned Veggies

 15 minutes 18 minutes 2

Ingredients

- 1 cup baby carrots
- 1 cup broccoli florets
- 1 cup cauliflower florets
- 1 tbsp olive oil
- 1 tbsp Italian seasoning
- Salt and ground black pepper, as required

Directions

1. Put all the ingredients in a bowl and toss to coat well.
2. Set the temperature of the air fryer to 380°F to preheat for 5 minutes.
3. After preheating, place the vegetable mixture into the greased air fryer basket.
4. Slide the basket into the air fryer and set the time for 18 minutes.
5. While cooking, flip the vegetables 2-3 times.
6. When the cooking time is completed, transfer the vegetable mixture onto serving plates.
7. Serve hot.

Nutrition: Calories: 76; Fats: 5.1 g; Carbohydrates: 5.9 g; Protein: 1.4 g

136
Balsamic Veggies

 15 minutes 18 minutes 2

Ingredients

- 1 tbsp olive oil & 1 tbsp garlic, minced
- 1 cup cauliflower florets
- 1 cup broccoli florets
- 1 cup zucchini, sliced
- ½ cup yellow squash, sliced
- ½ cup fresh mushrooms, sliced
- 1 small onion, sliced
- ¼ cup balsamic vinegar
- 1 tsp red pepper flakes
- Salt and ground black pepper, as required

Directions

1. Put all the ingredients in a large bowl and toss to coat well.
2. Preheat the air fryer to 400°F
3. After preheating, place the vegetable mixture into the greased air fryer basket.
4. Slide the basket into the air fryer and cook for 18 minutes.
5. While cooking, flip the vegetables once after 8 minutes. When the cooking time is completed, transfer the vegetable mixture onto serving plates. Serve hot.

Nutrition: Calories: 77; Fats: 5 g; Carbohydrates: 5.8 g; Protein: 1.8 g

137
Maple Glazed Veggies

 15 minutes 20 minutes 4

Ingredients

- 2 oz cherry tomatoes
- 1 large parsnip, peeled and chopped
- 1 large carrot, peeled and chopped
- 1 large zucchini, chopped
- 1 green bell pepper, seeded and chopped
- 6 tbsp olive oil
- 3 tbsp maple syrup
- 1 tsp Dijon mustard
- 1 tsp mixed dried herbs
- 1 tsp garlic paste
- Salt and ground black pepper, as required

Directions

1. Put the vegetables in a bowl with 3 tbsp of oil and toss to coat well.
2. Preheat the air fryer to 350°F to preheat for 5 minutes.
3. After preheating, place the vegetable mixture into the greased air fryer pan.
4. Slide the basket into the air fryer and cook for 20 minutes.
5. Flip the veggies after 8 minutes of cooking.
6. Meanwhile, in a bowl, add the remaining oil, maple syrup, mustard, herbs, garlic, salt, and black pepper and mix well.
7. After 15 minutes of cooking, put the maple syrup mixture in the pan with vegetables and mix until well combined.
8. When the cooking time is completed, transfer the vegetable mixture onto serving plates.
9. Serve hot.

Nutrition: Calories: 293; Fats: 21.4 g; Carbohydrates: 22.8 g; Protein: 2.3 g

138. Stuffed Eggplants

 15 minutes 8 minutes 2

Ingredients

- 4 small eggplants, halved lengthwise
- 1 tsp fresh lime juice
- 1 tsp vegetable oil
- 1 small onion, chopped
- ¼ tsp garlic, chopped
- ½ small tomato, chopped
- Salt and ground black pepper, as required
- 1 tbsp nutritional yeast
- ¼ green bell pepper, seeded and chopped
- 1 tbsp tomato paste
- 1 tbsp fresh cilantro, chopped

Directions

1. Carefully cut a lengthwise slice from one side of each eggplant.
2. With a small spoon, scoop out the flesh from each eggplant leaving a thick shell.
3. Transfer the eggplant flesh into a bowl.
4. Drizzle the eggplants with lime juice evenly.
5. Set the temperature of the air fryer to 320°F and preheat for 5 minutes.
6. After preheating, arrange the hollowed eggplants in the greased air fryer basket.
7. Slide the basket into the air fryer and set the time for 3 minutes.
8. Meanwhile, in a skillet, heat the oil over medium heat and sauté the onion and garlic for about 2 minutes.
9. Add the eggplant flesh, tomato, salt, and black pepper and sauté for about 2 minutes.
10. Stir in the nutritional yeast, bell pepper, tomato paste, and cilantro and cook for about 1 minute
11. Remove the pan of veggie mixture from the heat.
12. When the cooking time is completed, transfer the cooked eggplants onto a plate.
13. Stuff each eggplant with the veggie mixture.
14. Close each eggplant with its cut part.
15. Again, preheat the air fryer to 355°F.
16. After preheating, arrange the stuffed eggplants in the greased air fryer basket.
17. Slide the basket into the air fryer and set the time for 8 minutes.
18. When the cooking time is completed, transfer the eggplants onto a platter.
19. Serve warm.

Nutrition: Calories: 156; Fats: 2.3 g; Carbohydrates: 26.8 g; Protein: 7.1 g

139
Green Beans & Mushroom Casserole

 15 minutes 12 minutes 2

Ingredients

- 24 oz fresh green beans, trimmed
- 2 cups fresh button mushrooms, sliced
- 3 tbsp olive oil
- 2 tbsp fresh lemon juice
- 1 tsp ground sage
- 1 tsp garlic powder & 1 tsp onion powder
- Salt and ground black pepper, as required
- ⅓ cup French fried onions

Directions

1. Put the green beans, mushrooms, oil, lemon juice, sage, and spices in a bowl and toss to coat well.
2. Preheat the air fryer to 400°F
3. After preheating, place the mushroom mixture in the greased air fryer basket.
4. Slide the basket into the air fryer and set the time for 12 minutes.
5. While cooking, shake the mushroom mixture occasionally.
6. When cooked, top with fried onions and serve.

Nutrition: Calories: 321; Fats: 17.6 g; Carbohydrates: 34.1 g; Protein: 5.3 g

140
Beans & Rice Stuffed Bell Peppers

 15 minutes 15 minutes 4

Ingredients

- ½ small bell pepper, seeded and chopped
- 1 (15-oz) can diced tomatoes with juice
- 1 (15-oz) can red kidney beans, rinsed and drained
- 1 cup cooked white rice
- 1 ½ tsp Italian seasoning
- 4 large bell peppers, tops removed and seeded
- ½ cup nutritional yeast

Directions

1. In a bowl, mix together the chopped bell pepper, tomatoes with juice, beans, rice, and Italian seasoning. Stuff each bell pepper with the rice mixture.
2. Set the temperature of the air fryer to 320°F to preheat for 5 minutes.
3. After preheating, arrange the bell peppers into the greased air fryer basket.
4. Slide the basket into the air fryer and set the time to 15 minutes.
5. After 12 minutes of cooking, top each bell pepper with nutritional yeast.
6. When the cooking time is completed, transfer the bell peppers onto a serving platter.
7. Set aside to cool slightly. Serve warm.

Nutrition: Calories: 242; Fats: 2.2 g; Carbohydrates: 40.9 g; Protein: 14.5 g

141
Rice & Veggie Stuffed Tomatoes

 15 minutes   22 minutes   2

Ingredients

- 4 large tomatoes
- 1 tsp olive oil
- 1 carrot, peeled and finely chopped
- 1 cup frozen green peas, thawed
- 1 onion, chopped
- 1 garlic clove, minced
- 2 cups cooked cold white rice
- 1 tbsp soy sauce
- 6 cup fresh baby kale

Directions

1. Cut the top of each tomato and scoop out the pulp and seeds.
2. In a skillet, heat the oil over low heat and sauté the carrot, peas, onion and garlic for about 2 minutes.
3. Stir in the soy sauce and rice and remove from the heat.
4. Stuff each tomato with the rice mixture.
5. Set the temperature of the Air fryer to 355°F to preheat for 5 minutes.
6. After preheating, arrange the tomatoes into the greased air fryer basket.
7. Slide the basket into Air fryer and set the time for 20 minutes.
8. When the cooking time is completed, transfer the tomatoes onto a serving platter.
9. Set aside to cool slightly.
10. Serve warm alongside the kale.

Nutrition: Calories: 206; Fats: 1.9 g; Carbohydrates: 40.2 g; Protein: 6.9 g

142
Oats & Beans Stuffed Bell Peppers

 15 minutes 16 minutes 4

Ingredients

- 2 large bell peppers, halved lengthwise and seeded
- 2 cups of cooked oatmeal
- 4 tbsp canned red kidney beans, rinsed and drained
- 4 tbsp coconut yogurt
- ¼ tsp ground cumin
- ¼ tsp smoked paprika
- Salt and ground black pepper, as required

Directions:

1. Set the temperature of the air fryer to 355°F to preheat for 5 minutes.
2. Arrange the bell peppers in the greased air fryer basket, cut-side down.
3. Slide the basket into the air fryer and cook for 8 minutes.
4. When finished, set the bell peppers aside to cool.
5. Meanwhile, in a bowl, add the oatmeal, beans, coconut yogurt, and spices and mix well. Stuff each bell pepper half with the oatmeal mixture.
6. Now, set the air fryer to 355°F to preheat for 5 minutes.
7. After preheating, arrange the bell peppers in the air fryer basket. Slide the basket into the air fryer and set the time for 8 minutes.
8. When the cooking time is completed, transfer the bell peppers onto a serving platter.
9. Set aside to cool slightly.
10. Serve warm.

Nutrition: Calories: 238; Fats: 3.5 g; Carbohydrates: 41.9 g; Protein: 9.5 g

143
Beans & Veggie Burgers

 15 minutes 21 minutes 3

Ingredients

- 1 cup cooked black beans
- 2 cups boiled potatoes, peeled and mashed
- 1 cup fresh spinach, chopped
- 1 cup fresh mushrooms, chopped
- 2 tsp chili lime seasoning
- Non-stick cooking spray
- 6 cups fresh baby spinach

Directions

1. Place the beans, potatoes, spinach, mushrooms, and seasoning in a large bowl and, with your hands, mix until well combined.
2. Make 4 equal-sized patties from the mixture.
3. Set the temperature of the air fryer to 370°F to preheat for 5 minutes.
4. After preheating, arrange the patties in the air fryer basket.
5. Slide the basket into the air fryer and cook for 19 minutes.
6. After 12 minutes of cooking, flip the patties.
7. Serve them alongside the spinach.

Nutrition: Calories: 198; Fats: 0.9 g; Carbohydrates: 38.2 g; Protein: 9.4 g

144
Veggie Fried Rice

 10 minutes 15 minutes 4

Ingredients

- 3 cups cooked cold white rice
- 1 ¼ cup frozen vegetables (carrot, corn and green peas)
- ⅓ cup soy sauce
- 1 tbsp olive oil

Directions

1. Put all the ingredients in a bowl and stir to combine.
2. Place the mixture into a baking pan.
3. Preheat the air fryer to 360°F
4. After preheating, put the baking pan into the air fryer basket.
5. Slide the basket into Air fryer and set the time for 15 minutes.
6. While cooking, stir the rice mixture after every 4 minutes.
7. When cooking time is completed, transfer the rice mixture onto a platter.
8. Serve hot.

Nutrition: Calories: 215; Fats: 3.9 g; Carbohydrates: 38.6 g; Protein: 5.8 g

145
Chickpeas Falafel

 15 minutes   30 minutes   3

Ingredients

- 2 cups dried chickpeas, soaked overnight and drained
- 1 onion, chopped
- ¾ cup fresh flat-leaf parsley leaves, chopped
- ¼ cup fresh cilantro leaves, chopped
- 2 garlic cloves, minced
- 1 tbsp chickpea flour
- 2 tsp ground cumin
- 2 tsp ground coriander
- 1 ½ tsp sea salt
- 1 tsp ground black pepper
- ½ tsp cayenne pepper
- 9 cup fresh baby greens

Directions

1. In a food processor, add all the ingredients and pulse until a coarse mixture is formed.
2. Transfer the mixture into a bowl.
3. With your hands, make equal-sized balls from the mixture.
4. Set the temperature of the air fryer to 370°F to preheat for 5 minutes.
5. After preheating, arrange the falafel balls into the greased air fryer basket in 2 batches.
6. Slide the basket into air fryer and set the time for 15 minutes.
7. Flip the falafel balls once halfway through.
8. When the cooking time is completed, transfer the falafel balls onto serving plates.
9. Serve alongside the baby greens.

Nutrition: Calories: 151; Fats: 1.9 g; Carbohydrates: 23.7 g; Protein: 9.8 g

146
Tofu in Orange Sauce

 15 minutes 10 minutes 4

Ingredients

For Tofu:
- 1 pound of extra-firm tofu, pressed and cubed
- 1 tbsp cornstarch
- 1 tbsp low-sodium soy sauce

For Sauce:
- ½ cup water
- ⅓ cup fresh orange juice
- 1 tbsp maple syrup
- 1 tsp orange zest, grated
- 1 tsp garlic, minced
- 1 tsp fresh ginger, minced
- 2 tsp cornstarch
- ¼ tsp red pepper flakes, crushed
- Ground black pepper, as required

Directions

1. Put the tofu, cornstarch, and soy sauce in a bowl and toss to coat well.
2. Set the tofu aside to marinate for at least 15 minutes.
3. Preheat the air fryer to 390°F.
4. After preheating, arrange the tofu cubes in the greased Air fryer Basket.
5. Slide the basket into the air fryer and set the time for 10 minutes.
6. While cooking, flip the tofu cubes once halfway through.
7. Meanwhile, for the sauce: In a small pan, add all the ingredients over a medium-high heat and bring to a boil, stirring continuously.
8. Remove from the heat and transfer the sauce into a large bowl.
9. When the cooking time is complete, transfer the tofu cubes into the bowl with the sauce and gently stir to combine.
10. Serve immediately.

Nutrition: Calories: 152; Fats: 6.7 g; Carbohydrates: 11.5 g; Protein: 11.7 g

147
Tofu with Cauliflower

 15 minutes   15 minutes   4

Ingredients

- 1 ½ (14-oz) block firm tofu, pressed and cubed
- ½ small head cauliflower, cut into florets
- 1 tbsp nutritional yeast
- 1 tbsp canola oil
- 1 tsp ground turmeric
- ¼ tsp dried parsley
- ¼ tsp paprika
- Salt and ground black pepper, as required

Directions

1. Put all of the ingredients into a bowl and mix well.
2. Set the temperature of the air fryer to 390°F to preheat for 5 minutes.
3. After preheating, arrange the tofu mixture in the greased air fryer basket.
4. Slide the basket into the air fryer and set the time for 15 minutes.
5. Shake the basket once halfway through.
6. When the cooking time is completed, transfer the tofu mixture onto a platter.
7. Serve hot.

Nutrition: Calories: 134; Fats: 8 g; Carbohydrates: 4.7 g; Protein: 11.2 g

148
Tofu with Broccoli

 15 minutes   15 minutes   3

Ingredients

- 8 oz firm tofu, pressed, drained and cubed
- 1 head broccoli, cut into florets
- 1 tbsp olive oil
- 1 tsp ground turmeric
- ¼ tsp paprika
- Salt and ground black pepper, as required

Directions

1. Mix together all the ingredients in a bowl.
2. Preheat the air fryer to 390°F.
3. After preheating, arrange the tofu mixture in the greased air fryer basket.
4. Slide the basket into the air fryer and cook for 15 minutes.
5. Toss the tofu mixture once halfway through.
6. When the cooking time is completed, transfer the tofu mixture onto serving plates.
7. Serve hot

Nutrition: Calories: 124; Fats: 7.3 g; Carbohydrates: 6.1 g; Protein: 8.8 g

149
Classic Fried Pickles

20 minutes | 10 minutes | 2

Ingredients

- 1 egg, whisked
- 2 tbsp buttermilk
- ½ cup fresh breadcrumbs
- ¼ cup Romano cheese, grated
- ½ tsp onion powder
- ½ tsp garlic powder
- 1 ½ cups dill pickle chips, pressed dry with kitchen towels

Mayo Sauce:

- ¼ cup mayonnaise
- ½ tbsp mustard
- ½ tsp molasses
- 1 tbsp ketchup
- ¼ tsp ground black pepper

Directions

1. In a narrow bowl, whisk the egg with buttermilk.
2. In another bowl, mix the breadcrumbs, cheese, onion powder, and garlic powder.
3. Coat the pickle chips in the egg mixture, then, in the breadcrumbs
4. Cook in the preheated air fryer at 400°F for 5 minutes; shake the basket and cook for 5 minutes more.
5. Meanwhile, mix all the sauce ingredients until well combined. Serve the fried pickles with the mayo sauce for dipping.

Nutrition: Calories: 404; Fats: 24.5 g; Carbohydrates: 32.5 g; Protein: 14.1 g

150
Japanese Tempura Bowl

20 minutes | **10 minutes** | **3**

Ingredients

- 1 cup of all-purpose flour
- salt and ground black pepper, to taste
- ½ tsp paprika
- 2 eggs
- 3 tbsp soda water
- 1 cup panko crumbs
- 2 tbsp olive oil
- 1 cup of green beans
- 1 onion, cut into rings
- 1 zucchini, cut into slices
- 2 tbsp soy sauce
- 1 tbsp mirin & 1 tsp dashi granules

Directions

1. Mix the flour, salt, black pepper, and paprika in a shallow bowl. In a separate bowl, whisk the eggs and soda water. In a third shallow bowl, combine the panko crumbs with olive oil.
2. Dip the vegetables in the flour mixture, then in the egg mixture; lastly, roll over the panko mixture to coat evenly.
3. Cook in the preheated air fryer at 400°F for 10 minutes, shaking the basket halfway through the cooking time. Work in batches until the vegetables are crispy and golden brown.
4. Then, make the sauce by whisking the soy sauce, mirin, and dashi granules. Bon appétit!

Nutrition: Calories: 446; Fats: 14.7 g; Carbohydrates: 63.5 g; Protein: 14.6 g

151
Crispy Roasted Broccoli

 45 minutes   15 minutes   2

Ingredients

- ¼ tsp Masala
- ½ tsp red chili powder
- ½ tsp salt
- ¼ tsp turmeric powder
- 1 tbsp chickpea flour
- 2 tbsp yogurt
- 1-pound broccoli

Directions

1. Cut the broccoli into florets. Soak in a bowl of water with 2 tsp of salt - for at least half an hour - to remove impurities.
2. Take the broccoli florets out of the water and let them drain. Pat them down thoroughly with kitchen roll.
3. Mix all of the other ingredients to create a marinade.
4. Toss the broccoli florets in the marinade. Cover and chill for 15-30 minutes.
5. Preheat the air fryer to 390°F. Place the marinated broccoli florets into the fryer. Cook for 10 minutes.
6. 5 minutes into cooking, shake the basket. Florets will be crispy when done.

Nutrition: Calories: 73; Fats: 1.3 g; Protein: 5.7 g; Carbohydrates: 9.5 g

152
Crispy Jalapeno Coins

 10 minutes   10 minutes   8 to 10

Ingredients

- 1 egg
- 2-3 tbsp coconut flour
- 10 sliced and seeded jalapenos
- A pinch of garlic powder
- A pinch of onion powder
- A pinch of Cajun seasoning (optional)
- A pinch of pepper and salt

Directions

1. Preheat your air fryer to 400°F.
2. Mix all of the dry ingredients.
3. Pat the jalapeno slices dry. Dip the 'coins' into the egg wash and then into the dry mixture. Toss to thoroughly coat.
4. Add the coated jalapeno slices to the air fryer in a single layer. Spray them with olive oil.
5. Cook them until they are just crispy.

Nutrition: Calories: 83; Fats: 4.1 g; Protein: 4,7 g; Carbohydrates: 6.9 g

153
Cauliflower Casserole

 10 minutes   15 minutes   6

Ingredients

- 1 cauliflower head, cut into florets and boil
- 1 cup cheddar cheese, shredded
- 1 cup mozzarella cheese, shredded
- 2 oz cream cheese
- 1 cup heavy cream
- 1/2 teaspoon pepper
- 1/2 teaspoon salt

Directions

1. Put cream in a small saucepan and bring to a simmer. Stir well. Add cream cheese and stir until it thickens.
2. Remove from the heat and add 1 cup of shredded cheddar cheese. Season and stir well.
3. Place the boiled cauliflower florets into the greased baking dish.
4. Pour the mixture from the saucepan over cauliflower florets.
5. Sprinkle the mozzarella cheese over the cauliflower mixture.
6. Select 'Bake' mode.
7. Preheat to 375°F
8. Place the baking dish in the air fryer basket and bake for 15 minutes.
9. Serve and enjoy.

Nutrition: Calories: 201; Protein: 8.3 g; Fats: 17.6 g; Carbohydrates: 3.7 g

154
Artichoke Hearts

 10 minutes 35 minutes 2

Ingredients

- ½ cup arrowroot flour (gluten-free & easily digestible)
- 1 tbsp organic herb de Provence
- 1-2 eggs
- 1 bag of frozen artichoke hearts
- Cooking spray

Directions

1. In a clean bowl, mix a cup of arrowroot flour with Herb de Provence. Mix well.
2. Take another bowl and make an egg wash by whisking 1-2 eggs.
3. Take each artichoke and dip it in the egg mixture followed by the flour mixture. Try to make sure that there is a generous coating!
4. Coat the air fryer basket with oil and place the artichokes inside.
5. Allow them to cook for 15 minutes using the chips feature.
6. Flip the artichokes after about 7 minutes using tongs.
7. Serve and enjoy.

Nutrition: Calories: 164; Protein: 5.5 g; Fats: 4.3 g; Carbohydrates: 25.7 g

155
Basil Eggplant Casserole

 10 minutes 35 minutes 6

Ingredients

- 1 eggplant, sliced
- 3 zucchini, sliced
- 4 tablespoon basil, chopped
- 1 tablespoon olive oil
- 3 garlic cloves, minced
- 3 oz mozzarella cheese, grated
- 1/4 cup parsley, chopped
- 1 cup grape tomatoes, halved
- 1/4 teaspoon pepper
- 1/4 teaspoon salt

Directions

1. Place all ingredients in a large bowl and toss well to combine.
2. Pour the eggplant mixture into the greased baking dish.
3. Select 'Bake' mode.
4. Preheat to 350°F.
5. Bake for 35 minutes.
6. Serve and enjoy.

Nutrition: Calories: 94; Protein: 4.2 g; Fats: 5.5 g; Carbohydrates: 6.8 g

156
Brussels Sprouts and Broccoli

Ingredients

- 1 lb broccoli, cut into florets
- 1 lb Brussels sprouts, ends cut
- 1 teaspoon paprika
- 1/2 onion, chopped
- 1 teaspoon garlic powder
- 1/2 teaspoon pepper
- 3 tablespoon olive oil
- 3/4 teaspoon salt

Directions

1. Put all ingredients into a mixing bowl and toss well.
2. Spread the vegetable mixture in a baking dish.
3. Select 'Bake' mode.
4. Preheat to 400°F
5. Bake for 30 minutes
6. Serve and enjoy.

Nutrition: Calories: 103; Protein: 2.5 g; Fats: 6.7 g; Carbohydrates: 9.9 g

157
Easy Frizzled Leeks

Ingredients

- ½ tsp porcini powder
- 1 ½ cup rice flour
- 1 tbsp vegetable oil
- 2 medium-sized leeks, sliced into julienne strips
- 2 large-sized dishes with ice water
- 2 tsp onion powder
- Fine sea salt, to taste
- Cayenne pepper, to taste

Directions

1. Allow the leeks to soak in ice water for about 25 minutes; drain well.
2. Put the rice flour, salt, cayenne pepper, onion powder, and porcini powder into a resealable bag. Add the leeks and shake to coat well.
3. Drizzle the vegetable oil over the seasoned leeks. Air fry for 18 minutes at 390°F; turn them halfway through the cooking time.
4. Serve with homemade mayonnaise or any other sauce for dipping. Enjoy!

Nutrition: Calories: 145; Carbohydrates: 27.3 g; Fats: 2.7 g; Protein: 3.2 g

158
Fried Green Beans with Pecorino Romano

 15 minutes   10 minutes   3

Ingredients

- 2 tbsp buttermilk
- 1 egg
- 2 tbsp cornmeal
- 1 tbsp tortilla chips, crushed
- 2 tbsp Pecorino Romano cheese, finely grated
- 2 tbsp coarse salt and crushed black pepper, to taste
- 1 tsp smoked paprika
- 4 oz green beans, trimmed

Directions

1. Whisk together the buttermilk and egg in a bowl.
2. Combine the cornmeal, tortilla chips, Pecorino Romano cheese, salt, black pepper, and paprika.
3. Coat the green beans in the egg mixture and then in the cornmeal. Next, place them in the lightly greased cooking basket.
4. Cook at 390°F for 4 minutes in the air fryer. Shake the basket and cook for a further 3 minutes.
5. Taste, adjust the seasoning and serve with the dipping sauce if desired. Bon appétit!

Nutrition: Calories: 156; Carbohydrates: 16.9 g; Fats: 6.7 g; Protein: 7.8 g

Chapter 10
21-DAY MEAL PLAN

DAY	BREAKFAST	LUNCH	DINNER
1	Ricotta Muffins	Beef Steak Kabobs with Vegetables	Asian-Inspired Swordfish Steaks & Sweet-and-Sour Mixed Veggies
2	Sweet Baked Avocado	Air Fryer Chicken Wings & Spicy Green Beans	Bacon Wrapped Pork Tenderloin & Corn on the Cob with Herb 'Butter'
3	Rhubarb Pie	Asian Sesame Cod & Roasted Broccoli with Sesame Seeds	Juicy Lamb Chops & Basil Tomatoes
4	Pancakes	Balsamic Glazed Chicken & Spicy Roasted Potatoes	Tofu with Cauliflower
5	Tofu Scramble	Easy Tuna Wraps	Stevia Lemon Garlic Chicken & Lemony Spinach
6	Sweet Corn Fritters with Avocado	Lamb and Creamy Brussels Sprouts	Lemon Scallops with Asparagus
7	Baked Eggs	Salmon with Fennel and Carrot	Flavored Rib Eye Steak & Sweet Potato Cauliflower Patties
8	Homemade Muffins	Rice & Veggie Stuffed Tomatoes	Pork Shoulder with Pineapple Sauce & Glazed Broccoli
9	Lemon Pie	Chinese Steak and Broccoli	Rosemary Lamb Chops & Hasselback Potatoes
10	Cocoa Pudding	Pork Tenderloin with Bell Peppers	Soy Chicken and Sesame & Soy Sauce Mushrooms

11	Tofu Scramble	Spicy Cajun Shrimp & Spiced Sweet Potatoes	Beef Korma Curry
12	Chia Pie	Pork Fillets with Serrano Ham & Kale with Pine Nuts	Ginger and Green Onion Fish & Sesame Seeds Bok Choy
13	Blueberry Muffins	Chicken Fajitas with Avocados	Veggie Fried Rice
14	Lemon Biscotti	Tuna and Fruit Kebabs	Pork Spare Ribs & Carrot with Zucchini
15	Sweet Baked Avocado	Mustard Marinated Beef, Green Beans with Carrots	Spicy Chicken Meatballs & Potato with Bell Peppers
16	Pancakes	Mini Turkey Meatballs & Veggie Ratatouille	Breaded Hake with Green Chili Pepper and Mayonnaise
17	Sweet Corn Fritters with Avocado	Mesquite Pork Chops & Buffalo Cauliflower Wings	Beans & Rice Stuffed Bell Peppers
18	Homemade Muffins	Herbed Chicken Marsala	Baked Lemon Pepper Chicken Drumsticks & Spicy Potatoes
19	Pancakes	Fish and Vegetable Tacos	Roast Beef & Green Beans & Mushroom Casserole
20	Lemon Pie	Oats & Beans Stuffed Bell Peppers	Chilean Sea Bass with Green Olive Relish & Maple Glazed Veggies
21	Rhubarb Pie	Tofu with Broccoli	Beef with Mushrooms

CLAIM YOUR AMAZING FREE BONUS
WITH THIS QR CODE

DOWNLOAD THE FULL COLOR EDITION
WITH THIS QR CODE

Made in United States
North Haven, CT
19 February 2023